BOUNTY

Ten Ways to Increase Giving
at Your Church

Kristine Miller & Scott McKenzie

Abingdon Press

Nashville

Bounty
Ten Ways to Increase Giving at Your Church

Library of Congress Cataloging-in-Publication Data has been requested.

ISBN 978-1-4267-6597-1

Unless otherwise noted, Scripture quotations are taken from the New Revised Standard Version of the Bible, copyright 1989, Division of Christian Education of the National Council of the Churches of Christ in the United States of America. Used by permission. All rights reserved.

Scripture quotations marked NIV are taken from the Holy Bible, New International Version®. NIV®. Copyright © 1973, 1978, 1984 by Biblical, Inc.™ Used by permission of Zondervan. All rights reserved worldwide. www.zonervan.com. The "NIV" and "New International Version" are trademarks registered in the United States Patent and Trademark Office by Biblica, Inc.™

Scripture quotations marked ESV are from The Holy Bible, English Standard Version®, copyright © 2001 by Crossway Bibles, a publishing ministry of Good News Publishers. Use by permission. All rights reserved.

Scripture quotations marked NRSV are from the New Revised Standard Version of the Bible, copyright 1989, Division of Christian Education of the National Council of the Churches of Christ in the United States of America. Used by permission. All rights reserved.

13 14 15 16 17 18 19 20 21 22—10 9 8 7 6 5 4 3 2 1

MANUFACTURED IN THE UNITED STATES OF AMERICA

To our spouses, Joni and Bret,
who demonstrate bountiful generosity every day.
We are grateful for your love, support, and patience in the
writing of this book and in everyday life.

CONTENTS

INTRODUCTION

As a form of ministry, fundraising is as spiritual as giving a sermon, entering a time of prayer, visiting the sick, or feeding the hungry.
Henri Nouwen, *The Spirituality of Fundraising*

Tears ran down Steve's face as he stood before his congregation and shared his stewardship story. He had accepted the job of stewardship campaign chair simply because "if the pastor asks me to do something, I usually do it." Little did he know how being part of a stewardship campaign would change his life. For Steve, it all began with gratitude. Until now, he had never really stopped to think about how he had been blessed and how God's hand had led him from growing up as the child of an addicted single mother, through medical school, and on to a life filled with a loving family and very successful medical practice. "Everything I have comes from God, and with great joy we will be giving the largest gift we have ever given in our lives. And truthfully, it won't be enough."

Now is the time to reconsider your stewardship message, moving it from financial to spiritual, from mundane to missional, from painful to inspirational. *Bounty* will enable you to lead your congregation on a journey that will not only raise money for your ministry, but also grow your congregation spiritually in the process.

Through our combined thirty-plus years of working with churches, we understand that well-intentioned people with little or no experience are often charged with the seemingly insurmountable task of raising funds to cover the budget. Perhaps you find yourself faced with this exact charge. Now that you have accepted the job, you surely will be told about previous failed efforts, how the budget has been dramatically reduced and is now at a bare minimum. All you need to do is get people to increase their giving so your church can finally afford to fix the leak in the roof and give your staff their first raise in years. The finance committee is waiting in the wings, preparing to finalize next year's budget, which shows an increase of 25 percent over last year. And of course, over the last three years there has never been an increase in giving greater than 2 percent. As a member of the stewardship committee, it is expected that when all the pledges are in, you will begin developing a year-round stewardship program, even though no one can really describe to you what that means. Miracles are expected to happen under your leadership, and you have no idea where to begin.

In spite of stories such as these, there are *other* stories— stories you will find in these pages that will transform how you approach stewardship in your church. Whether or not you knew it when you accepted the position, the role of stewardship advocate is a vital one. Your role is to carry the banner of stewardship and invite others to join in the march. Clergy and laity who are charged with increasing awareness, understanding, and practice of solid stewardship principles carry a substantial responsibility—one that also brings satisfaction and reward beyond measure. The task at hand is challenging (Kingdom building always is!), but your work is holy work and has the potential to change you and your congregation forever. Your service will liberate those who are weighed down

2

by their own wealth, and your efforts will change the hearts of those who want to live out God's will rather than their own. Through your faithfulness, church members will deepen their faith. Lives will be enriched. The ministry will transform.

Our goal for writing *Bounty* was to honor and support stewardship advocates over the years in the churches we served. We now extend that same honor and support to you, so that the insights and practices found in *Bounty* will be effective for you and your church. *Bounty* envisions stewardship to be grounded in gratitude, revealed in prayer, lived in faith. *Bounty* offers the only approach to stewardship development that truly works long term—a *spiritual* one. At the forefront, it entails seeking God's guidance for the use of the blessings we have been given, bringing us closer to God. This God-given inspiration moves us from searching for the right annual campaign program, or the perfect sermon, to an entirely new way of thinking about who we are and what we are called to do. By incorporating the practices of *Bounty*, you will lead your church family to experience the genuine joy of generosity.

The ten best practices described in *Bounty* will guide you in your stewardship role. These practices will challenge you to replace ineffective number crunching with prayerful discernment. Both clergy and laity will benefit from *Bounty's* explanation of how old habits can inadvertently sabotage efforts to raise money for ministry. In addition, *Bounty's* teachings show how certain conversations, such as ones about tithing, can help or hurt your stewardship efforts. The examples we include here are drawn from our experiences; the practical tools we provide will help to lighten your load.

We've yet to hear anyone on a stewardship committee say they thought their job was easy. It's not. Achieving all that God desires for you and your stewardship ministry requires a focused and intentional effort from you, your committee, and your entire church membership. You may even find yourself bucking traditions, eliminating long-standing unhealthy practices, moving out of your comfort zone, and, perhaps at times, being the lone advocate for stewardship and bountiful generosity. Yours is a sacred and significant responsibility. Know that we are rooting for you and, more important, so is our Creator.

Blessings on the journey,

Kristine and Scott

Chapter One

INVITE GOD INTO THE MIX

Stewardship is a journey that is grounded in gratitude,
revealed in prayer, lived in faith.
Kristine Miller and Scott McKenzie

Churches that want to experience the bounty of generous giving must redefine the concept of stewardship. *Bounty* envisions stewardship as grounded in gratitude, revealed in prayer, and lived in faith. Each of these vital elements of stewardship is necessary for growing faithful and generous stewards in your church.

The first step on the journey is a return to our roots, where we reemphasize the main difference between secular and church fundraising. While there is much to be learned from secular, nonprofit fundraising models, we should never forget who we are as the church. We are God's people engaged in doing God's work. Real bounty, real generosity occurs when we are mindful of our most vital partner on the journey: God. Church members with experience in nonprofit fundraising often say to us, "Look, can't we just tell people what we need them to give?" As tempting as that might seem, stewardship is not about what we want people to give, but about what *God* wants his people to give. And truthfully, God's number is always higher than any number a consultant or fundraiser might suggest.

Brenda was a beloved member of her congregation and the person who was the first to volunteer for any task. When her church began its capital campaign, Brenda was the first to jump in and begin to consider the amount of her gift. Not a person of great wealth, but living comfortably, Brenda was considering a $15,000 contribution, which she felt was reasonable and appropriate for her circumstances. However, over the course of the campaign, Brenda was encouraged to consider the concept of gratitude. She began to think about how she had been blessed by God. Now a widow, Brenda had been married to the love of her life for more than fifty years. She had a lovely home where her three grandchildren often visited and was a part of a vibrant Christian community. Her life was full, and her heart became filled with gratitude. As a result, Brenda's gift increased to $25,000. Brenda was pleased and comfortable with this new amount as well. Then Brenda did something she had never done before. She began to pray about her giving, asking God, "What would you have me do?" Looking back, Brenda said, "Be careful if you pray that prayer, because God will answer. And the answer almost always takes you out of your comfort zone." Brenda ended up giving $40,000, a gift that required much faith and was not necessarily all that comfortable, but she felt it was what God had called her to do.

Brenda invited God into the mix, and the result was bountiful generosity and a changed heart. Yes, Brenda could have been told what to give, and she might have given it, but in the end it would not have changed her heart or her relationship with God. Inviting God into the mix begins with a fundamental shift in how we look at our possessions, the world, and ourselves. Henri Nouwen expresses this in *The Spirituality of Fundraising* by saying, "Fundraising is . . . always a call to conversion. . . . To be converted means to experience a shift in how we see and think and act."

Indeed, Brenda experienced conversion. What if our stewardship campaigns were not about balancing budgets, but rather about shifting hearts toward God? How can we change the way we approach stewardship and help people experience a conversion leading to bountiful giving? The conversion Brenda experienced was the result of a stewardship journey based on gratitude, prayer, and faith.

Inviting God into the Mix through Gratitude

Piglet noticed that even though he had a very small heart,
it could hold a rather large amount of gratitude.
A. A. Milne, *Winnie the Pooh*

Dr. Robert Emmons, professor of psychology at the University of California in Davis and a researcher in the psychology of gratitude, says:

Herein lies the energizing and motivating quality to gratitude. It is a positive state of mind that gives rise to the passing on of the gift through positive action. As such, gratitude serves as a key link in the dynamic between receiving and giving. It is not only a response to kindnesses received, but it is also a motivator of future benevolent actions on the part of the recipient.[1]

To create and cultivate a culture of gratitude in your church, the first task is to help people realize the many blessings they have received from God. Instead of distributing spreadsheets, line-item budgets, and then pledge cards, you should begin by distributing gratitude cards. Before asking for a single dollar or pledge, ask people, "How have you been blessed? What are the gifts in your life for which you are grateful to God?" You need to find a variety of ways to creatively and intentionally invite people to remember, reflect, and respond with gratitude. For example, Tyler Weig of Des Moines, Iowa, caused a chain reaction resulting in an overflowing of gratitude and generosity. Tyler decided to donate a kidney to whoever could use it.[2] His incredible act of altruism started a chain of events that resulted in five families being forever changed. The lucky recipient of Tyler's kidney was Lance Beyer. His wife was an incompatible donor for Lance, but her kidney went to another patient in need. This continued until five people, with a total of twelve years on the transplant waiting list, ended up with healthy kidneys and lives free from dialysis. One of the men wanted to help a friend but wasn't compatible, so he gave his kidney to a complete stranger. He said he made the sacrifice because "it's kind of what you do. You've got two . . . share your spare." A grateful heart has no choice but to overflow with generosity.

Inviting God into the Mix through Prayer

> *Let gratitude be the pillow upon which you*
> *kneel to say your nightly prayer.*
> Maya Angelou

Inviting God into the stewardship mix begins with expressions of gratitude and then requires an invitation to a deeper life of prayer and openness to the spirit of God. Let's return to our story of Brenda. Brenda began her journey with gratitude. Then Brenda began to ask a very scary but potentially life-changing question: "God, what would you have me do?" Brenda invited God into the mix through a willingness to be open to the leading of God's spirit. Brenda would say her giving and her life were radically changed.

If gratitude reminds us of our blessings and their ultimate source, prayer is our willingness to allow those resources to be used by God. In fact, we believe *willingness* is the secret to spiritual growth and the key to truly bountiful, generous giving. Unfortunately, in our culture, people are more likely to project an attitude of self-accomplishment than cite divine providence, and this carries over into the church. It's easy to believe that good fortune is of our own doing rather than a result of God's blessings.

Mark liked to maintain control of every aspect of his life. During his church's stewardship campaign, Mark decided he would give, but only sparingly. After all, Mark had many reasons not to contribute. He and his wife were completely remodeling their home and planning several international vacations. At the same time, they were paying college tuition for both children. Mark knew what he could afford to give, and no one, not even God, was going to move him off that amount. To Mark's credit, even in the midst of his willfulness, he began the journey, taking into account his many blessings. His children had attended youth group, had been on mission trips, and were well on their way to being incredible people of faith. Mark then remembered how the pastor and church had stood beside him as he struggled through the slow and lingering death of his father from Alzheimer's.

Mark was a dedicated runner, and he often used his training time for prayer and reflection. As Mark ran and prayed, something began to change. Pretty soon, the house that "needed" remodeling was okay the way it was. Suddenly, the next big trip he and his wife had planned didn't seem quite so important. Mark's dream of retiring at fifty was put on hold. As a consequence, Mark and his wife ended up more than tripling their gift to the church. Not long after these radical decisions, Mark's wife related this comment to her church family with a laugh: "I've asked Mark to quit running. We can't afford any more prayer runs!" Mark had gone on the journey from willfulness to willingness through gratitude and prayer. Mark took a great risk and invited God into the mix.

The opposite of being willful is being *will-less*. A will-less person is someone who says, "I can't give. I've surrendered to the financial constraints of my life, and I can't give." Since the economic recession of 2008, we have seen more people surrender to the spirit of will-lessness. In the last several years, we have heard countless people lay out an entire litany of reasons why they can't give. Truthfully, most are legitimate. These reasons include job loss, cuts in pay, having to support adult children, and high health-care costs. Yet there are also faithful individuals in our churches who follow God's leading rather than their own.

For example, Charlotte had every reason in the world to be will-less, to surrender to her circumstances and say, "I can't give." Charlotte was an elderly long-time church member who was on a fixed income. She had been careful with her finances over the years and now lived a comfortable life. Charlotte was also a committed tither. Unfortunately, when Charlotte became the victim of a scam, she lost most of her money. She ended up having to declare bankruptcy. Most anyone in a similar circumstance would have decreased giving to the church—but not Charlotte. Charlotte actually went before her bankruptcy judge to ask permission to continue her current pledge to her church. As Charlotte told her story, she radiated peace, joy, and hope instead of a spirit of fear, anxiety, and will-lessness. Charlotte invited God into the mix, and the result was bounty and generosity.

Inviting God into the Mix through Faith

*Take the first step in faith. You don't have to see
the whole staircase, just take the first step.*
Dr. Martin Luther King, Jr.

Gratitude and prayer are mere spiritual platitudes if they
are not combined with the phrase *lived in faith*. Bountiful,
generous giving will occur only when pastors and leaders are
willing to model what it means to live and give in faith. Only a
leader who is modeling faithful living and bountiful giving has
the right to challenge others to step out and join him or her.
When looking at a church's giving list, we are amazed at how
often those who serve in financial and administrative leadership positions are nowhere to be found. If our leaders are giving
at token levels, why should we expect anything different from
the people sitting in the pews? Does our giving reflect gratitude
and prayer? Does our giving reflect faith and a willingness to
stretch and step out of our comfort zone?

A stewardship campaign grounded in gratitude, revealed
in prayer, and lived in faith will affect people not only in
their giving but also in every aspect of life. A person should
consider all for which he or she is grateful, prayerfully determine how God would have him or her use these blessings,
and then ask, "Now what? How will I faithfully live this out?"
The answer may be the filling out of a financial pledge card
for the first time or increasing a current pledge. The answer
may be signing up and participating in a mission trip or Bible
study for the first time. Sometimes the answer may be vol-
unteering at a soup kitchen or homeless ministry. Sometimes
we have seen the "Now what?" be a momentous and truly
life-changing event, such as a call to ministry or a change of
vocation. Big or small, any response that emerges from a

grateful heart and is prayerfully determined and lived out in faith is an appropriate response—one to be celebrated and lifted up.

> He looked up and saw rich people putting their gifts into the treasury; he also saw a poor widow put in two small copper coins. He said, "Truly I tell you, this poor widow has put in more than all of them; for all of them have contributed out of their abundance, but she out of her poverty has put in all she had to live on." (Luke 21:1–4)

Invite God into the Mix: To-Do List

Gratitude

1. In worship, in small groups, or even on your website, share two- to three-minute videos or in-person gratitude talks by a variety of people of diverse ages.

2. Kick off your stewardship campaign with a Gratitude Sunday service. Following a sermon on gratitude, invite people to fill out cards on which they include all the blessings in life for which they are grateful to God. Have the children and youth complete gratitude cards the week before and post them for members to see as they arrive on Gratitude Sunday. Display the gratitude cards in a creative way. For example, one church created a gratitude tree, and the leaves of the tree were the multicolored gratitude cards.

3. Demonstrate and practice congregational gratitude. Instead of doing follow-up calls to people who didn't make a pledge, what about making gratitude calls to people who did make a pledge? So many churches are worried about offending someone by forgetting to

thank those who did give that they choose to thank no one and end up offending everyone.

4. In general, after every major congregational effort, church leaders should model expressing gratitude by calling and thanking volunteers and servants through an organized phone "thank-a-thon." Imagine the impact throughout the community if all the vacation Bible school helpers and teachers were called and personally thanked by members of the administrative board.

Prayer

1. Pastors and lay leaders should model and give witness to both the need for prayer and the power of prayer to move us to more bountiful and generous giving. Imagine the impact of having someone like Mark tell his story of how the power of prayer moved him, or the effect of hearing Charlotte tell of her willingness.

2. Expect church leaders and finance leaders to be people of prayer. So often, the most important quality we look for on finance and stewardship committees is a background in finance. Make sure your church leadership is full of prayer warriors.

3. Every stewardship campaign should be an opportunity to teach and practice prayer. Why not distribute and collect prayer commitment cards at the beginning of a stewardship campaign? The card can be as simple as the following:

      I promise to pray daily for:
      _____ My church
      _____ Our campaign
      _____ My gift

4. Distribute a daily devotional guide and invite people to pray daily. Included in the appendix of this book is a sample of a twenty-one-day devotional guide used by many of our churches. During worship opportunities, have leaders refer to the chosen devotional guide and ask them to share how it has affected their walk and their giving.

5. Provide opportunities for prayer throughout your stewardship campaign. Prayer vigils, Taize services, and prayer labyrinths all have been utilized by churches as a way to invite God into the mix. Intentionally invite groups within the church to participate in these prayer activities. Invite men's and women's groups, youth groups, Sunday school classes, shut-ins, and choirs to sign up for prayer activities.

Faith

1. On a monthly basis, ask individuals who have stepped out in faith to offer a witness and testimony as to how it has changed their lives in little or big ways. Don't limit this witness to financial giving, but don't exclude financial giving, either.

2. Ask people to step out intentionally, and give them many options and specific ways to respond affirmatively. We have heard so many sermons encouraging people to step out in faith, but so many seem to stop too soon and offer no real specific challenge. Don't forget to tell people how you want them to respond to the question "Now what?"

3. From leadership staff to new members, create a culture where people are routinely asked and expected to step out of their comfort zones when they serve and give.

Chapter   Two

....

ELIMINATE SECRECY SURROUNDING MONEY

A wise man should have money in his head,
but not in his heart.
Jonathan Swift

Bountiful giving requires a willingness to talk about money—inside the church and from the pulpit. Daring to talk about money is one of the most challenging aspects of any successful stewardship program. Both pastors and lay leaders struggle to have open and honest conversations about this issue. Often, the pastor has been pressured to keep talk of money out of the pulpit, usually by people who don't give, and has acquiesced. But when church leaders choose to keep silent about money, they allow money to hold their ministries hostage. Instead of addressing the topic head on, many churches back away, making money taboo and giving the issue an unhealthy measure of power. By talking about money and speaking clearly about its control of our lives, we can begin to put things back into perspective. Just as Jesus demonstrates his control over demons by asking them to name themselves (Luke

8:27–30), so must we talk about money to diffuse its power. In 1 Timothy 6:9–10, we are told, "But those who want to be rich fall into temptation and are trapped by many senseless and harmful desires that plunge people into ruin and destruction. For the love of money is a root of all kinds of evil, and in their eagerness to be rich some have wandered away from the faith and pierced themselves with many pains."

In society today, we often define success by what we own, rather than by who we are. This insatiable desire to acquire more drives people to idolize money and allow it to control their lives. A PBS program created the term "affluenza," defining it as "1. The bloated, sluggish and unfulfilled feeling that results from efforts to keep up with the Joneses. 2. An epidemic of stress, overwork, waste and indebtedness caused by dogged pursuit of the American Dream. 3. An unsustainable addiction to economic growth."[1] Until church leaders become intentional about eliminating the secrecy around money, the affluenza epidemic will continue, and they will be unable to inspire spiritually mature stewards who contribute generously to the church.

To understand the importance of money conversations, first we must concede that money has power and influence. In our society today, conversations about who has money, who needs money, and who is working or cheating to obtain money are pervasive. Occupy Wall Street-ers object to those who have amassed great amounts of money, and Tea Partiers object to being told by their government how to share their money. No matter what your political bent, it is impossible to avoid hotly debated opinions about money in our society. We seem to believe what we have or what we own defines who we are. Often in our society, there is shame or indignity in being without resources, and, likewise, it seems there is often embarrassment in having too many resources. While we may not fully understand our emotional and psychological connections to money, it is clear we have strong and often unhealthy attachments to our stuff. The challenge becomes even greater when money conversations move into the church. It is here where the level of discomfort becomes exponentially greater.

Often people say, "The preacher should just preach and keep the money talk out of it." For many clergy, this is reason enough not to preach about money. Clergy often feel as uncomfortable as their members about money conversations and are relieved no one wants to hear a "money" sermon. Why are clergy so generally ill-equipped to tackle money talk? One reason may be they have their own personal money issues. Often, mounting debt from school loans, credit cards, and mortgages add to the difficulty of open and honest money conversations. It is precisely because of this discomfort that the issues related to money must be addressed directly.

Consider some of the biblical principles surrounding the issue of money and personal finances. Jesus spoke of money and possessions more than any other topic. In fact, Jesus spoke about money more often than heaven and hell combined. Eleven of the thirty-nine parables are about money and possessions. Why was Jesus seemingly obsessed with money talk? Of course, Jesus was not concerned with having possessions, but he was concerned with people's attachments to their money and possessions. Jesus urged people to become less attached to their stuff and more attached to God. Jesus knew our obsession with money would prohibit us from living in a closer relationship with our Creator.

Consider the story of the Rich Young Ruler (Mark 10:17–27). Just as Jesus was leaving on a journey, a man of great wealth approached Jesus, fell at his feet, and asked what he needed to do to inherit eternal life. After keeping the commandments and leading a good life, the Rich Young Ruler wanted to know what else was needed to achieve life eternal. Jesus told him there was just one more thing—sell everything, give the profits to the poor, and follow Jesus. Because of his great wealth, the man was unwilling. He just had too much to lose. Jesus used this moment to teach his disciples (and us) by saying,

> "How difficult it will be for those who have wealth to enter the kingdom of God!" And the disciples were amazed at his words. But Jesus said to them again, "Children, how difficult it is to enter the kingdom of God! It is easier for a camel to go through the eye of a needle than for a rich person to enter the kingdom of God." And they were exceedingly astonished, and said to him, "Then who can be saved?" Jesus looked at them and said, "With man it is impossible, but not with God. For all things are possible with God." Mark 10:23-27 (ESV)

Jesus tells us we should put our trust in God rather than in our possessions. Dealing with the control money has over us allows us to develop a more healthy and spiritually rich relationship with God. The church can and should play an active role in this—starting with honest and open conversations about money.

In many of our churches, the secrecy around money extends all the way to the top. Clergy are willingly or unwillingly kept in the dark about who gives and how much they give. Frequently there is a policy (either written or simply understood) that the pastor should not and will not know what people are contributing to the ministries of the church. In these churches, lay leaders and pastors are typically in agreement that the policy is in the best interest of the congregation. Laity explain this "policy" by arguing that if a pastor knows how much people contribute, he or she might treat people differently. What people are really saying is they believe the pastor will treat those who give more with favoritism and those who give less with scorn. Members confide in their pastor about deeply personal issues, such as infidelity, mental and physical health concerns, and addictions, without questioning the pastor's ability to respond pastorally. But the church leadership draws the line when it comes to knowing how much a family contributes to the church. The supposition is the clergy just cannot be trusted to respond pastorally to money issues. This makes absolutely no sense and is usually a smokescreen for larger problems in the church. It is unreasonable to assume a pastor is capable of responding appropriately to the afflictions of her or his flock but unable to respond pastorally to their levels of giving. In churches with this policy, clergy and laity are complicit in keeping money issues in the dark, thereby crippling the church's ability to develop mature stewards.

For example, during the annual stewardship program at a church, the pastor sent a letter to his congregation detailing how much he and his family were planning to pledge in support of the ministries of the church. Because clergy salaries were published in the annual report, the congregation knew the percentage of his income (12 percent) and level of sacrifice this represented. The pastor's letter expressed gratitude to God for the many blessings he and his family had experienced. He spoke about their prayerful approach to determining the amount of their gift and how important it was to their spiritual development that they continue to return to God a portion of their blessings through the ministries of the church. This not only demonstrated the pastor practiced what he preached, but also helped to diminish the discomfort around money talk in the church.

In another church, a group of individuals (who always seemed at odds with the direction in which the church was going) plagued the pastor. Almost daily, the pastor received visits from church attenders and members who felt the music should be more upbeat, the youth program should be more vital, or the outreach budget should be increased. The pastor met opposition at every turn, causing her to become confused and concerned about how to lead the congregation effectively. When the policy was changed and the pastor was permitted to view the giving list, she found none of the outspoken families' names on it. Not one of those attempting to sabotage her ministry was giving anything to the church. They had freely offered their opinions but were not invested in the church's ministries. Rather than being committed to investing in God's vision for their church, they hid behind the policy of secret giving.

In some churches, pastors decide to keep the giving list at arm's length, settling on something of a middle ground. They know the hierarchy of those who contribute without knowing the actual amounts, or they know general amounts given without actually looking at specific numbers on the list. Frequently, they are at the mercy of the person who is entrusted with the giving list—often the bookkeeper—for information. There is no reasonable point to this model, which simply enforces the notion that giving records should be kept secret from the pastor while many private details about members are confided to the pastor.

For clergy to provide appropriate pastoral care, which is essential to a healthy church, the clergy must know the spiritual needs of church members. The generosity of members is one of the truest measures of spiritual health and should affect the type of pastoral care individuals receive. In other words, the pastor should care for people individually, based on each individual's spiritual needs—often made clear by their levels of giving. For example, if the pastor is aware of a family that is contributing $1,000 annually to the church and also owns a vacation home with a boat, has children in private school, and owns expensive cars, the pastor could reasonably conclude this family has not yet discovered the joy of generosity—or at the very least has not considered the church to be a priority for sharing God's bounty. Likewise, if a church member is contributing relative to her means, she may be helpful in teaching others about the joy of generosity. Without knowing the giving list, the pastor does not have the information required to offer the necessary and appropriate pastoral care. Giving information enables the pastor to minister according to the needs of each church member.

In some churches, tradition dictates that, rather than complete a pledge card, members keep their giving between God and themselves. Members are not asked to indicate how much they intend to give. While the decision about what to give should always be between the giver and God, the actual gift amount rarely remains between the giver and God. Someone tracks giving within the church. Someone at your church counts the money received in the offering plates. Someone may do your taxes for you, and surely someone at the Internal Revenue Service is keeping track of your charitable deductions. The truth is, rather than encouraging generosity, discouraging pledges typically results in low-level giving and satisfaction with the status quo. In contrast, pledges represent a prayerful, intentional, and faithful response to God's abundant blessings. By completing a pledge card (or arranging an ongoing electronic-funds transfer), people indicate a willingness to step out in faith to fulfill God's vision for their church. They have chosen to be deliberate and faithful in their giving. Pledges represent a level of accountability to God and to the church. Consider the other "pledges" that people make in life. Most people have a mortgage, student loan, car loan, credit card bill, or other type of financial commitment to which they contribute monthly. When a person claims, "I don't believe in pledging," what he or she is really saying is, "I don't believe in making a pledge to the church."

To eliminate the secrecy that surrounds money, church leaders must become more comfortable in their relationships with money and possessions. Begin by encouraging your governing body (for example, council, cabinet, trustees, session, and vestry) to discuss a series of questions centered on money and their relationships with money (see Eliminating Secrecy Surrounding Money: To-Do List, on page 23, for questions). Before the meeting, send the governing body this list of questions regarding attitudes and responses to money. During the first fifteen minutes of the meeting, invite the governing body to share their responses to the questions. At first, you may experience long pauses and uncomfortable silences, but eventually the ice will break and you will be amazed at the conversation that emerges. Often, these questions will open up incredibly honest and heartfelt sharing by people who feel trapped by debt and guilt over their low-level giving. Many people raised in churches have experienced coercion and manipulation to elicit higher levels of giving, and this type of discussion can liberate and help to unload damaging baggage. Anger, tears, and laughter help bond people together over the common challenges they face in regard to money and diffuse money's power and control over them. In one church, a woman who had been raised in a high-pressure church explained how she had been told repeatedly as a child that if she did not tithe, she would go to hell. She had fallen away from this church but remained angry and bitter every time she heard "money" sermons. Simply mentioning the word *tithe* gave rise to unpleasant memories and caused her to shut down. Her fire-and-brimstone experience had created a significant barrier to her understanding of stewardship and living a life of generosity.

It is vital to the long-term health of the church and your efforts to encourage bountiful giving so that conversations about money no longer are confined to budget and finance discussions. By inviting more honest, open, and frequent conversations about money, you will diffuse its power and enable your members to grow spiritually in a closer relationship to God.

Eliminating Secrecy Surrounding Money: To-Do List

1. **Personal Finance Program:** Invite your congregation to participate in a program to get their personal finances in order. Programs such as those offered by Dave Ramsey, Crown Financial Ministries, and Nathan Dungan will not only open the door to meaningful money conversations but also help people understand and adjust their money behaviors.

2. **Leadership Conversations:** Encourage your church's leadership to share personal observations and insights about money with each other. Begin by providing a few questions in advance of your next meeting. Let your leadership know you will be spending the first few minutes of your meeting responding to the questions. It is important not to force anyone to answer questions publicly. Many people have money baggage that is painful and deeply felt. Keep the floor open as long as possible, allowing people to share as they are

moved to do so. Some questions to ask include the following:

- Growing up, did you feel wealthy or poor? What was your family's attitude toward money? Did you worry about money?
- Do you feel money has power? Why? Why not?
- Do you believe your relationship with God is influenced by how much stuff you have?
- Has your self-esteem changed as your income has changed? How much does your income determine how you feel about yourself?
- Do you know others for whom money or income determines their sense of self-worth? How much does your personal self-worth depend on your income? How much does your personal self-worth depend on how much you give away?
- When and how were you introduced to the idea of giving to the church? Who taught you about it, and what did they say? What did you think about it?
- When was the first time you were asked (or expected) to make a charitable gift? How much did you give? What is your first memory of deciding to make a charitable gift, spontaneously and voluntarily? What inspired you to make the gift?
- How do you feel about your current level of charitable giving? How does it reflect your personal priorities?

3. **Preach about Money:** If you follow the church's lectionary, you will have ample material for your sermons. As previously stated, close to one-third of Jesus' parables address issues of money and possessions. Of course, Jesus never used guilt or pressure as a motiva-

tor but rather invited people to consider their blessings and how individual gifts can be used by God for God's purposes.

4. **Recruit Good Stewards:** As you consider filling leadership positions in the church, identify those whose giving reflects a strong commitment to your mission and ministry. This does not mean church leaders need to be the largest contributors, but giving should reflect a meaningful commitment relative to one's means.

Chapter Three

SET LEADERSHIP EXPECTATIONS

If your actions inspire others to dream more,
learn more, do more and become more,
you are a leader.
John Quincy Adams

Talented and committed leaders who have a clear understanding about their roles and who are prepared to fulfill them are essential to increasing giving in your church. Clergy and laity need to be chosen and recruited with clear expectations for their positions. Downplaying the importance of volunteer positions and minimizing expectations will only result in the declining interest of your leaders and failure of important ministry. Does your leadership consist of lovely people who happen to have some spare time on their hands, or have you recruited the most talented and committed leadership your congregation has to offer? Remember, the success and vitality of your congregation's ministry depend upon the success and vitality of your leadership.

Whom to Recruit

First, choose the right people for leadership positions. To be considered for a position on your governing board, a person should have demonstrated a history of contributing significantly to the ministries of your church. People serving in leadership positions will make key decisions regarding how the church's resources will be used to accomplish ministry objectives. Shouldn't they have a stake in the outcome? If your church's leadership is not financially supporting God's work through your church, why would anyone else be compelled to support it? Leadership candidates should not just be on record as givers; they should also make an annual commitment or pledge. By making a pledge, leaders indicate they consider giving to the church a priority, and they are willing to be accountable. This does not mean you need to recruit into leadership positions the largest contributors to your church, but potential leadership candidates should be intentional and faithful givers. Those calculating their contribution as a percentage of income with the goal of giving away 10 percent or more will be your most effective leaders. This implies, as indicated in chapter two, that the pastor is privy to the church's giving list. This will enable the pastor to identify individuals whose giving reflects the type of commitment necessary to serve in a leadership capacity. Those participating in church leadership should be seasoned stewards—spiritually mature leaders who embrace bountiful generosity.

Candidates under consideration for leadership positions on stewardship or finance committees should be well acclimated to the church and preferably members for at least one year. Many churches make the mistake of recruiting brand new members for leadership roles, assuming such a position will usher a new member into deeper involvement within the church. Often, a new member who has some sort of financial background is recruited immediately upon arrival to serve on the finance or stewardship committee. This is especially problematic if the new recruit is also new to the faith. Serving on stewardship or finance committees often exposes new people to the more mundane aspects of life in the church, which may result in their becoming disillusioned and leaving the church.

When nongivers, or even low-level givers, are chosen to head finance committees, it becomes difficult to inspire the congregation to higher levels of giving. When poor givers lead the stewardship committee, they inevitably enlist others who also lack the necessary gifts and skills to lead a successful stewardship process. Recruits tend to be those who are satisfied with low-level giving, see barriers to reaching goals everywhere they look, and perceive giving as reluctant submission rather than a spiritual practice of joyful generosity. For example, while meeting with a newly formed stewardship committee, one chair who happened to be a low-level giver suggested that, because the pastor would be retiring soon and the economy was in decline, the stewardship process should include a "soft ask." In the view of this chair, a soft ask meant mailing to the congregation an overview of the budget with the suggestion that if people could just give what they gave last year, that would suffice. She went on to defend her proposal by saying, "People are giving all they can. It wouldn't be right to ask them to give more." This was a church in steep decline—financially and otherwise—located in a suburban community where the average household income exceeded $250,000. The median pledge to the church was approximately $1,200. Actually, what the stewardship chair was saying was that *she* was unwilling to give more. She was not capable of taking the congregation on a spiritual journey to bountiful giving because *she* was unwilling to make the journey herself. We have yet to see a church where people are giving all they can, but we *have* seen that people consistently give as much as their leadership expects them to give. Ultimately, people who are not good stewards will never be bold and effective in leading others to be good stewards. Their lackluster giving models lackluster giving, and the stewardship process simply falls flat. By contrast, recruiting people who practice bountiful giving will provide a healthy foundation on which to build stewardship efforts.

Recruiting Leaders and Setting Expectations

How you invite people into leadership roles will have a significant impact on the success of your ministry. During our extensive experience as church consultants (and church members), we have frequently seen volunteer roles downplayed, and as a result, the moderate to poor abilities of those filling the positions seems inevitable. While people often joke about being nominated to serve as the chair of their stewardship committee during a meeting in which they happened to be absent, this is often painfully the case. Churches tend to recruit less rigorously, settling instead for warm bodies to fill volunteer positions. We often hear, "If expectations are set too high, people won't serve, and the responsibilities will default to the staff or no one at all. So we post positions in the church bulletin, hoping and praying that someone will call the office and volunteer." Prospective volunteers are told the position is not very time consuming and shortcuts can certainly be taken, giving the message that expectations for results are low. The assumption is that low expectations will lead to a larger group of volunteers to serve the church. These volunteers may not accomplish much, but at least all the service slots will be filled.

Not only can this be detrimental to the current ministry, but residual effects could last for many years, setting the ministry back considerably. For example, in one church we served, a volunteer was handed the church directory and asked to begin calling until all the positions for Sunday school teachers were filled. No consideration was given to the specific skills needed to be a Sunday school teacher—anyone would do. This obviously is not the best approach for recruiting a talented and committed team of Christian educators.

When recruiting for leadership roles, it is important to communicate to candidates what gifts and skills are needed to be successful in the role, as well as clear long-term expectations. To fulfill the mission of the church and grow its ministries, cultivate the most talented, focused, and devoted leadership team possible. If the position requires ten hours per month, tell your candidate this, without apologies. If the position requires people with pastoral-care skills, select people with these skills and let them know this is why you have chosen them. Whenever possible, leaders should be recruited in person by the pastor or other church leader. Sending out a fill-in-the-blank letter or posting the position in your bulletin probably will not lead you to the most gifted and able person to fill the position. Soft selling the requirements will only disgruntle your volunteers and guarantee you will be rejected the next time you try to recruit them. The work you are doing is important—boldly tell your volunteers what is at stake. Jesus admonished his disciples, and us, to share the good news! This is life-changing work, and it deserves your very best. Those who consider taking on leadership roles need to understand the importance of the task they are being asked to fulfill as well as how they will be asked to lead. Not only will they need to accomplish their specific ministry objectives, but they will also need to serve as role models for your congregation. For example, if someone is serving as the lay leader in your church, shouldn't it be expected that he or she be in worship regularly? Shouldn't it be expected that the leadership is praying daily for the church and its ministries? Shouldn't it be expected that leadership be invested in the ministries of your church through the annual budget? Shouldn't it be expected that your leadership be willing to witness to others about their journey as stewards? People, especially busy people, want clear, specific, unwavering expectations before they make a commitment. They also want to spend their precious time accomplishing tasks that make a difference. Once on board, these leaders will provide the model for others to follow and enable your church to fulfill its ministry objectives.

Leadership Begins at the Top

Leaders don't create followers. They create more leaders.
Tom Peters

Bountiful generosity and vibrant ministry will occur when the pastor is willing to lead by example. Even if the stewardship committee does a superb job designing a great fall appeal, it will not be successful without the leadership of the pastor. One church stewardship committee decided to "do this without the pastor"—handle everything related to the stewardship campaign without including the pastor. They felt the pastor was not in a position to share his stewardship witness due to a recent decrease in his pledge to the church. Over the past several years, the pressure of teenagers in high school and wanting to keep up with the lifestyle of the local community had caused the pastor and his family to lose sight of their priorities. The escalating demands of their lifestyle had forced the pastor's family into significant debt, which eventually led to a decrease in their financial support of the church's ministries. The stewardship committee did what they could to lead a stewardship process, but without the proper leadership from the pastor, their efforts fell substantially short. It is imperative that the pastor, as the spiritual leader of the church, give witness and model good stewardship. The church community needs to hear how leaders are leading, and living. They need to know that those whose leadership decisions influence the ongoing ministries of the church are indeed supporting those same ministries.

Even more unfortunate about this particular situation is the lost opportunity for the congregation to rally in support of their pastor and his family, and encourage them to overcome their financial dysfunction. Imagine what would have happened if this pastor had shared his burden with the congregation and let them know of his family's struggles. Imagine if he had shared his regret about getting caught up in the secular desire to acquire more and seek comfort and status through material things. Imagine if the pastor had said that, through prayer, he and his family had developed a plan to change their spending habits, pay off their debts, and increase their giving to the church. Many people find themselves coping with the very situation that this pastor and his family encountered. What a gift this pastor could have given to his congregation if he had been willing to let go of the shame he was experiencing and lead his congregation by example.

During another church's capital campaign, the pastor's leadership was clearly influential in achieving successful results. The pastor was asked to share her story at a campaign-leadership team meeting. She talked about the many blessings she had experienced over the past twenty years in ministry with her congregation. She reflected on the physical and spiritual support she received during her struggle with breast cancer and other family crises. She spoke from the heart about how much she loved serving as pastor. Then she said that every time she and her husband determined an amount as their gift to the capital campaign, they would ask God, "Is this enough?" With a glint in her eye, she said, "After asking that question several times, the answer was no, not yet." Eventually, this pastor and her husband, who were already tithing to the annual budget, made a pledge of $25,000 to their church's capital campaign. Their personal expression of gratitude, journey with God in prayer, and faithful response to God's leading was a profound witness and blessing to the congregation.

Leaders Lead and Witness

Leadership involves finding a parade and getting in front of it.
John Naisbitt

Your leadership must be prepared to lead the way, carry the banner, and inspire others to join the parade. One of our churches wanted to encourage people to give electronically. The entire governing board stood before the congregation and told them they had signed up for electronic giving and hoped others would follow. Then they played a video of the ninety-year-old church matriarch telling everyone how she had just signed up for electronic giving. She said, "If I can do it, so can you!" This kind of leadership inspires others to join the parade.

Finding opportunities for leadership to share their enthusiasm and support for church ministries is key to getting others to follow. Invite your stewardship committee or lay-leadership board to write a statement of expectations. In some churches, this may involve a commitment to tithing as a requirement of leadership. In others, it may be less rigorous, such as an obligation to calculate the percentage of income a person gives to the church with an expectation of eventually giving a contribution of 10 percent. It may take several months to build consensus around this statement of expectations, but the conversations leading to its adoption will be well worth the effort. Once the statement has been adopted, invite the members of your congregation to sign on to it, too. This can be done in a very literal sense, with the statement being presented to the congregation on foam board along with the signatures of your leadership. Congregation members may also sign the board, indicating their support of the statement.

Unfortunately, when leadership fails to "carry the banner," the result can be devastating. In one instance, church leadership spent months enthusiastically discussing plans to build a large and expensive multipurpose space to be used for increased programming for children and youth. When asked about his willingness to support this project financially, the lay leader of the church declared, "We have several wealthy families here that I am sure will carry the load." How can we expect the person in the pew to give with bountiful generosity when leaders refuse to step up and lead? What if you were told the pastor, finance chair, and lay leader in your congregation were not willing to make a substantial gift to the annual budget? Would you be willing to support it? It is important that the person selected as stewardship chair, as well as other leadership positions, be invested in the ministry of the church and living a generous life. Remember that the levels of giving will never rise above the levels given by your church leadership. Whom you choose to lead your efforts will determine what resources you will have to grow your ministries.

Steve Jobs said this about leadership: "Be a yardstick of quality. Some people aren't used to an environment where excellence is expected." The commitment of your leaders to excellence in their service to God and to your church should motivate others to become more engaged in your ministries. Setting the bar high for your leadership will convey the importance of the work God has for your church. The vibrancy of your ministry depends on it.

Set Leadership Expectations: To-Do List

1. Use the leadership board and stewardship committee meetings as an opportunity for spiritual growth and building community by incorporating a book study, time of devotion, or opportunity for reflections. Some resources we recommend:
   a. Henri Nouwen's *Spirituality of Fundraising* (available through various online resources)
   b. Scott McKenzie's *The Journey Begins*, a twenty-one-day devotional guide (available through Horizons Stewardship at horizonstewardship.com)
2. Before enlisting church leadership, consider the gifts and skills needed for the position. Invite God to guide you to someone who will fill that role well. When approaching a potential volunteer (preferably in person), speak honestly and clearly with him or her about the level of commitment needed to fulfill the task, without downplaying the time commitment or expected results. Let the potential volunteer know what gifts and skills you perceive are needed to achieve success in the position. Invite him or her to pray before making a decision.
   a. When new officers are elected, have them stand in front of the congregation and affirm their willingness to be leaders in the area of giving and bountiful generosity.

b. Statements of expectations may include other areas of discipleship in addition to giving. In some congregations, the notion of contributing to the life of the church through prayers, presence, gifts, service, and witness is communicated. Preaching about and sharing the importance of commitments to these areas within the church will enhance your success. A sermon series, one concept per week, is a great way to share this with the congregation. In addition, have a lay person talk about how he or she is faithfully living out his or her commitment through daily prayer, attendance in worship, sharing of talents, Christian witness, and service to the church and community.

Chapter Four

TITHE ONE ON

Now faith is the assurance of things hoped for,
the conviction of things not seen.
Hebrews 11:1 (ESV)

Discussions on giving to the church eventually lead to conversations about tithing. One of the most talked about and controversial topics is whether people should be expected to tithe—give 10 percent of their income to the church. Simply mentioning the tithe typically evokes myriad emotions and a flurry of debate. While most mainline churches agree the tithe is the biblical minimum standard for giving, the majority of Christians do not actually donate anywhere near 10 percent of their income. Additionally, those who contribute to churches also typically give to nonprofit charities, thereby reducing the percentage of income the church actually receives. Even in churches where the tithe is emphasized, members give significantly less than 10 percent of their income.

The denomination with the highest percentage of income is the Mormon church, whose members give away, on average, 5.2 percent of their income, of which 0.5 percent is given to charities outside the church.[1] Presbyterians, Episcopalians, United Methodists, Lutherans, and Roman Catholics give, on

TOTAL GIVING AS A SHARE OF INCOME BY RELIGIOUS AFFILIATION
Sorted by Gift Total as a Percentage of Income

	Percentage Giving	Mean Total Gift	Mean Religion Gift	Total Gift as Percentage of Income	Religion Gift as Percentage of Total Gift	Religion Gift as a Percentage of Income
Mormon	90.6	$4,078	$3,665	5.2	89.9	4.7
Other Protestant	69.0	$2,134	$1,137	3.5	53.3	1.0
Pentecostal/ASG	61.9	$1,282	$1,106	3.4	86.3	2.9
Muslim/Buddhist	49.2	$2,091	$587	2.8	28.1	0.8
Baptist	64.2	$1,302	$1,014	2.6	77.9	2.0
Jewish	91.8	$2,837	$1,129	2.3	39.8	0.9
Episcopal	82.6	$1,573	$868	2.0	55.2	1.1
Presbyterian	84.1	$1,349	$727	1.8	53.9	1.0
Lutheran	77.9	$1,230	$760	1.7	61.8	1.1

Source: Patrick Rooney, *Religious Giving*. Edited by David H. Smith, Indiana University Press, 2010, p. 5.

TOTAL GIVING AS A SHARE OF INCOME BY RELIGIOUS AFFILIATION, cont.

Sorted by Gift Total as a Percentage of Income

	Percentage Giving	Mean Total Gift	Mean Religion Gift	Total Gift as Percentage of Income	Religion Gift as Percentage of Total Gift	Religion Gift as a Percentage of Income
Methodist	69.6	$1,107	$680	1.6	61.5	1.0
Catholic	68.7	$1,083	$549	1.5	50.7	0.8
None	52.6	$642	$203	1.1	31.6	0.4
Jehovah's Witness	66.4	$358	$257	0.9	71.7	0.7
Missing	56.9	$552	$292	0.9	52.8	0.5
Greek/ Russian/ Eastern Orthodox	95.9	$479	$255	0.8	53.3	0.4

average, between 1.5 and 2 percent of income to church and charities. About half of their philanthropic contributions go toward the ministries of the church, resulting in the church receiving between 0.7 and 1 percent of their members' incomes. According to TENS (The Episcopal Network for Stewardship, www.tens.org), only 5 percent of people give away 10 percent of income, and 50 percent of those who attend church contribute nothing at all. The Barna Group, in a 2011 study, concluded the number of tithers is even less, declining to 4 percent of the adult population, the lowest level in the past ten years.[2] While the doctrine of most mainline churches includes giving 10 percent of income, studies indicate most church members do not practice tithing.

So why even consider the tithe? Will encouraging the tithe increase giving to the church? Why not ignore the tithe, as it does not seem to have caught on? What relevance could such an ancient tradition hold for us, and how should we talk about it?

Before we discuss tithing as a way to increase giving to your church, it is important to answer up front the questions that frequently derail conversations about tithing. First, it is not particularly helpful to debate whether a tithe is figured before or after taxes. Good and reasonable arguments may be made on both sides. More often than not, people who ask this question want a response that includes a legalistic viewpoint they can argue against (thus throwing out the tithe altogether). In our experience, the answer to this question makes absolutely no difference. In reality, if those who believed in tithing on income after taxes did so and those who believed in a before-tax tithe did so, there would be millions of dollars available to build God's kingdom today. Second, it is not particularly helpful to debate whether the tithe refers to giving to church and charities or just to the church. A concept referred to as the "new tithe" emerged several years ago and promotes "tithing" that includes churches and charities doing good works. In Roman Catholic parishes, members are often encouraged to give 5 percent to their church and 5 percent to charities; however, overall giving by Roman Catholics remains at 1.5 percent of income. Again, if church members chose to give away 10 percent of income to worthy causes—churches and charities—God's mission would be well funded and there would be no need for stewardship consultants or this book. The point is that most challenges to the concept of tithing arise from a fear of not having enough. Individuals who protest against the tithe may never have given away 10 percent of income. Arguing the finer points of tithing may be an interesting way of gaining insight into what stewardship baggage people are carrying, but it will do little to grow stronger stewards.

Holding up the tithe as the minimum standard of giving does have an important place in stewardship discussions, however. Not wishing to embark on a theological debate on the tithe, our perspective is based more on our experience as tithers and learning from other tithers. We have discovered there is something that changes fundamentally when a person begins to tithe. Concerns about who has what and arguments over how to divvy up pieces of the pie evaporate. Tithers are more likely to ask, how much will it take? rather than, how much can I take? In our experience, we have never met anyone who is a former tither. People who have embraced tithing often consider going beyond the tithe. One pastor told the congregation she and her husband currently gave 20 percent of their income away and had a personal goal of reaching 50 percent. Their dream was to give away as much as they kept for themselves. Those who have experienced tithing have a different view of the world. They get excited about giving away more and are grateful for the opportunity to share what they have been given with others. One of the great stewardship advocates of our time, Bruce Rockwell, said about his tithing conversion, "What I've learned from my own personal experience is that God does not need the tithe. I need it. I benefit from it. I've drawn closer to God through this spiritual discipline, this holy habit. I've learned more about God. I've experienced God's love and God's grace through the tithe."[3]

Every tither we know has the following traits in common:

1) An incredible sense of gratitude
2) A feeling of awe about how God has blessed them and their families
3) A spirit of generosity that permeates their lives
4) A perception of well-being
5) A desire to give away more

Those who give away 10 percent (or more) of their income to church and charity typically are reluctant to blow their own horns. However, tithers can provide incredibly moving and inspiring testimonies that significantly enlighten others who are still on the journey. These stories will inspire and encourage others, but only in the proper context with the appropriate audience. Tithers understand bountiful generosity and have been blessed by the practice of this holy habit. Tithers offer witness to giving from a place of gratitude, prayerfully discerning God's will for the resources they have been given and faithfully living out God's will rather than their own. They are incredible models for Christian stewardship and a blessing to your ministry.

So, here is where it gets tricky. How do you communicate your stewardship messages to a congregation where you know giving is, on average, less than 2 percent of their income? How do you lift up the concept of tithing to a congregation that would need to increase giving exponentially in order to do as you suggest? The answer is that you need to communicate different messages to members of your congregation based on where they are on the journey. This is key to your church's growth in giving and experiencing God's bounty.

In general, people fall into one of five categories:

1) **Tithers** have already discovered the joy of generosity and will likely continue to give generously, giving away 10 percent or more of their income.

2) **Proportional givers** have made a conscious decision to determine their giving based on a percentage of income with a personal goal of reaching a level of giving away 10 percent or more. Proportional givers have made the shift in priorities by choosing to be intentional and giving away the first of their income rather than what is left over.

3) **Flat-amount contributors** determine their giving based not on a percentage of income but on a flat amount. The amount of their contribution is usually determined based on a predetermined weekly or monthly amount. When reviewing your giving list, these flat-amount contributors are easily identified, because their annual contribution is divisible by 12 months or 52 weeks. In some cases, the amount is simply a flat $500 or $1,000 and is likely to have been the same for the past several years. Flat-amount contributors settle on an amount and do not waiver from it, year after year. Flat-amount contributors have not established stewardship as a priority in their lives and consider their gift to the church to be similar to dues or a tax.

4) **Token contributors** are often new to the faith (or new to your church) and have little awareness or history of charitable giving. Often, they contribute via the offering

plate rather than making an annual pledge to the church. Token contributors may attend worship sporadically and participate in very little else. They are unaware of how the church functions, and sometimes they believe the judicatory body (for example, synod, presbytery, annual conference, and diocese) provides funding for the local church rather than the other way around. Token contributors often become obstacles when placed in leadership roles because of their inexperience.

5) **Zero contributors** include one-third to one-half of all members in a typical mainline church, and as the name indicates, zero contributors contribute nothing. While this is obviously not ideal, it is considered the norm. Zero contributors are long-time members who may believe their volunteer efforts make up for their lack of financial contributions (they hear time, talent, *or* treasure rather than time, talent, *and* treasure). Or, they may be young confirmands who have not been taught about stewardship by either parents or confirmation instructors. They may be folks who have a superficial relationship with your church and are just beginning (or have not yet begun) their spiritual journey.

Clearly, people in each of the above categories perceive giving differently. A one-size-fits-all stewardship message actually will be an ill fit for all categories. Although it may require more planning and preparation, tailoring messages for each of these five groups within your congregation will result in a much more successful stewardship program.

The first group, the tithers, are already contributing 10 percent or more of their income to the church as an integral part of their journey as Christ's disciples. However, it is vitally important that the tithers' contributions continue. Remember, numerous nonprofits are vying for your members' attentions. First, be sure you are thanking tithers for supporting your ministries and the trust they are exhibiting in your ability to use their gifts well. The pastor should meet with tithers on a regular basis, to thank them and let them know how their gifts are used to further God's work through your church. At the very least, the pastor should write personal thank-you notes. Furthermore, use every opportunity to communicate your church's vision for ministry and your plans for accomplishing it. Let your donors know their tithes are just as effective in building God's kingdom as their gifts to other charities. Major donors often diminish or withdraw support from organizations when they feel disconnected. Be sure to keep your tithers in the loop, and they will continue to be engaged and invested in your ministries.

The second group, proportional givers, is the most likely to be significantly affected by the message of tithing. Proportional givers are committed to giving a percentage of their income with the goal of contributing 10 percent. The blessings of tithing, shared by one of their fellow parishioners, will likely encourage this group to continue their journey toward the tithe. Invite your proportional givers to a small group gathering in someone's home. After a bit of social time, have one or two of your tithers share stories about the blessings that tithing has brought to their lives. Invite others to share stories about how gratitude for God's abundant blessings has inspired them to greater levels of generosity.

In some churches, we have seen the pastor encourage proportional givers to try out the tithe for three months or more, which has resulted in success. Proportional givers may sometimes get stuck on their way to becoming a 10 percent giver, and a trial tithe is a helpful way to give them momentum. To an individual giving 3 or 5 percent, increasing giving to a full 10 percent can seem daunting. Encouraging the same individual to tithe for a trial period may be the very avenue needed to take a leap of faith and begin to tithe. For, once the trial period has ended, many will continue to contribute 10 percent, as they will have seen God provide for their needs and experienced the joy of generosity. After agreeing to give away 10 percent for three months, one church member said,

> A trial tithing experience is a wonderful way to test the waters, while opening one's life to so many blessings. Amazingly—and I truly mean this—amazingly, there was always enough. [The trial tithe] did make me more aware of how I was spending. I acknowledged that I was spending more frivolously than I had thought and reined in some of that to be able to meet the tithe.

To institute the trial tithe, you may want to include a line on your pledge card that says, "Is your pledge determined as a percentage of your income?" This will give you a target group for sending trial-tithe correspondence. In addition, spend several weeks sharing stories from tithers via e-mail, video, or direct mail. Culminate your activities with a special dinner for proportional givers at someone's home. Pray together and invite the proportional givers to try out tithing for three months. Be sure to follow up with those who choose to make this leap of faith. Afterward, you will want to hear about their experiences and share their testimonies.

Unlike those of the first two groups, members of the third group, the flat-amount contributors, are at the beginning of their giving journey. They have at least begun by making some gift to the church on an annual basis. Often, this group can be motivated in two ways: by comparing their current giving to the church to other expenditures in their lives and by encouraging them to calculate the percentage of income they are currently contributing. Let's examine your median contributor, who is giving somewhere around $1,040 annually, or $20 per week. How does this gift compare to the other financial commitments this family has made? For example, what does this household spend for cable television? How does the impact of the church on their lives compare with the value of cable programming? What does this household spend on luxuries such as wine, vacations, or fine dining? Is the amount spent on any of these items a better investment than the ministries of your church? How much are your members currently spending on their children's hockey, or lawn service, or pizza, or cell phones, or shoes? According to *Cosmopolitan* magazine, women own an average of seventeen pairs of shoes each. Men own an average of twelve pairs. Encourage your flat contributors to count the number of shoes in their closets and compare the value of these shoes to what they are currently contributing to your church. Ideally, you will be building consciousness of how people are making decisions about their resources and enlightening them as to how their resources may be put to better use.

Once they have been enlightened, invite these folks to calculate the percentage of income they spend on some typical household items (for example, coffee or entertainment) as well as what they give to your church. Provide a table that calculates giving levels at 1 percent to 15 percent at various income levels appropriate for your congregation. Encourage them to become proportional givers, contributing a percentage of income that reflects their gratitude for God's blessings and the importance of the ministries of your church.

The fourth and fifth groups, token and zero contributors, are the most challenging, as they have yet to embark on the stewardship journey. In many churches, these groups become the main focus, as they tend to make up a significant percentage of the congregation. Because these groups are sedentary in their giving, it won't be easy to make a significant breakthrough with them, but there are some messages that may get them moving. For these groups, the message of tithing may be so far beyond their comprehension that you are likely to do more harm than good by promoting it. These are also the people who often complain, "All the church does is talk about money." In return, talk about giving as a response to the blessings they have received from God. We have all received abundant blessings from a generous God, but token and zero contributors probably have never thought about life in that way—they have not fully understood that all of life is a gift from God. Help them to see that self, life, breath, relationships, and wealth are all gifts from a generous and loving God. Until they fully understand this concept, they will not have embarked on the stewardship journey. Cultivating a spirit of gratitude will create a desire to return to God a portion of the blessings received. While it is unlikely they will take you up on it, it is always helpful to remind people about the need to pray for God's guidance in giving. Invite these folks to take the very first steps on the journey of stewardship, focusing on gratitude for God's abundant blessings.

One way to communicate to each group of contributors effectively is to identify individuals who have moved beyond a certain level of giving. In a small group setting, invite these individuals to tell their personal giving stories to peers, identifying how they worked through the challenges to increase giving.

You may have noticed that none of the previously described appeals involves sharing the church's budget and requesting that people fund it. The reason is simply that this approach does not work for anyone, even though it is the method most commonly used by churches today to attempt to motivate their members to grow in generosity. It is tempting to think that if people only knew how much the church needed, they would step up and provide it. This is completely false. Although people in all previously identified categories are concerned about accountability and want to be assured the church leadership is fiscally responsible, they will not grow in giving based on an appeal to fund the church's growing expenses. Instead, create a ministry budget that demonstrates the ways in which the resources of your congregation are directly affecting lives in your community.

Typically, a ministry budget divides all church expenses among five categories: worship, pastoral care, communication, outreach, and Christian education. Distribute overhead such as salaries, utilities, and other expenses among these categories proportionately, to show how these line items from your budget support the ministries of your church. The ministry-focused budget is your opportunity to tell the story of your growing ministry and the impact you are making on members and the community you serve. This will help tithers and proportional givers feel good about their investment in your ministry. It will enlighten your flat-amount contributors by showing the value of their contribution to your church. For those who are just beginning their giving journey, it will help them understand how the amount of their contribution can significantly affect people's lives through your ministries.

Tithe One On: To-Do List

1. Plan now to share different messages with different groups based on giving history. Examine your giving list and place each household into one of the five

groups identified in this chapter. Develop a strategy for each group based on where they are on the stewardship journey. Consider various ways in which you might share the specific message tailored to meet the needs of each group. Small-group gatherings, one-on-one conversations, e-mail, video, and direct mail are some ways in which you can share your messages.

2. Develop a ministry-focused budget and share it, rather than a line-item budget.

3. Preach, teach, and talk about stewardship as a journey that is grounded in gratitude, revealed in prayer, and lived in faith. Lift up the tithe as a minimum standard for giving, but remember that most of your members are contributing about 2 percent of their income to giving, and 50 percent of that 2 percent goes to charities outside of your church.

4. During your annual appeal, intentionally focus on one or two of the five groups each year. Tailor your process and messages around the needs of the groups to which you are appealing.

5. Talk about tithing with couples during premarital counseling.

6. Invite those who are new members to participate in giving. Hand out pledge cards and set clear expectations about giving.

7. Create a proportional giving chart using annual income amounts appropriate for your congregation. Use it to motivate flat-amount contributors to be more intentional in calculating their giving as a percentage of their income.

PROPORTIONAL GIVING CHART

Annual Income	2%	4%	6%	8%	10%	12%	15%
$30,000	$600	$1,200	$1,800	$2,400	$3,000	$3,600	$4,500
$40,000	$800	$1,600	$2,400	$3,200	$4,000	$4,800	$6,000
$50,000	$1,000	$2,000	$3,000	$4,000	$5,000	$6,000	$7,500
$75,000	$1,500	$3,000	$4,500	$6,000	$7,500	$9,000	$11,250
$100,000	$2,000	$4,000	$6,000	$8,000	$10,000	$12,000	$15,000
$125,000	$2,500	$5,000	$7,500	$10,000	$12,500	$15,000	$18,750

STOP THE INSANITY

Chapter Five

Insanity: doing the same thing over and over again and expecting different results.
Attributed to Albert Einstein

Cultivating bountiful generosity requires intentional year-round planning that develops leadership, a compelling mission and vision, and a willingness to talk about money. It should result in making sure people are encouraged to go on a journey of gratitude, prayer, and faith. Sometimes the cultivation of generosity and giving requires that certain practices (which may be widely accepted but inherently counterproductive and unhealthy) be stopped. Healthy, fruitful giving calls for a willingness to sometimes just say *no*. What are some of the common practices we see in churches that must be stopped if we are going to experience an increase in giving and stewardship?

Insanity: Giving Amounts Published in Bulletin

How many times have you sat down in your pew, opened the bulletin, and, there in black and white, seen the following?

Dollars given for the past week: _____
Dollars given for the year: _____
Amount needed weekly: _____
Needed year-to-date: _____

Throughout the year, the numbers in these blanks are red, and people are led to believe that the church is on the verge of financial ruin. In fact, when the numbers are *quite* low, they appear in red bold type within a ruled box—impossible to miss. Then comes December, the Christmas offering, and somehow, miraculously, the year is finished either in the black or close to it. But come the following January, the scare tactics start all over again. Someone on the finance committee decides that the best way to encourage people to give is to scare them with impending financial doom.

When you publish the giving dollars in this manner, your regular attenders simply stop believing the numbers and, in turn, stop trusting the financial leaders of the church. Finance committee members are seen as Chicken Littles running around saying, "The sky is falling! The sky is falling!" We train our regular givers not to believe their leaders or take seriously their pleas for money.

The figures are simply misleading. Income for churches never comes in fifty-two equal installments. You should not take the budget and simply divide it by either fifty-two weeks or twelve months. In reality, many churches receive as much as 15 to 20 percent of their income in the month of December.

According to J. Clif Christopher in *Not Your Parents' Offering Plate*,[1] one of the leading reasons people decide to give to an organization is the organization's financial stability and fiscal responsibility. When we publish our giving dollars with a "woe is us" message, we completely undercut our perceived reputation as a financially stable and fiscally responsible organization.

The other significant problem with publishing giving amounts is the effect these numbers have on visitors and potential new members. Why would they want to join an organization that continually seems to be on the verge of going out of business? In his book *Wit, Wisdom & Moxie*, Jerold Panas says, "Tests emphatically demonstrate that citing the problems and challenges your organization faces is far less effective than talking about your opportunities, results and successes. . . . Donors want to hear the good news, positive outcomes, and results that count. That's what will keep them giving. Don't talk about your needs."[2]

So how do we let people know where we stand financially? Look at the last five years of giving records and determine what percentage of contributions historically comes in during each month. Determine whether you are ahead or behind based on the five-year average. For example, if, during the month of January, you typically have received 5 percent of the budget, and this year, you have received 6 percent of the budget, you are ahead. If you simply divided the budget by twelve months or 8.3 percent, you would actually be reporting to the congregation and visitors a deficit that isn't accurate. And, you would not be telling the truth. The sky is not falling. Stop the insanity of publishing giving amounts in the bulletin.

Insanity: Treating Everyone the Same

A very good friend of ours told us the story of an end-of-year letter he received from his church. This friend is one of the top three givers in his church. The letter went something like this:

Dear Friend,

We do live in uncertain and difficult economic times. Just as you may be struggling so is your church. Giving for the year is down, and like many people around the country, we are struggling to pay our bills. Last February our heating bills were X amount. And of course, you remember the two snowstorms that hit us on two separate Sundays. For the first time in many years we have been unable to pay our conference apportionments. Our finance committee met, and we have decided to ask each family to please consider giving two weeks' worth of regular giving over and above what you regularly give. If each of us does this we will end the year strong. Thank you.

Sincerely,
Pastor
Finance Chair

Our friend said he took that letter, crumpled it up, and threw it in the trash. Why? Here is what he told us:

As one of their top givers, I guess I'm not even important enough for them to send me a personal letter but just a form letter. They never thanked me for my donations, and they never gave any thought that for me to give two extra weeks is huge, after all I tithe. And I didn't miss those two weeks because I give electronically. Somebody who just throws two dollars in the plate—they are being asked to throw in four bucks—big deal. I'm tired of being taken for granted and tired of carrying a bunch of deadbeats. Guess I'm not very Christian but that is just how I feel.

An identical form letter sent to everyone treats everyone equally, but not fairly. In talking with pastors and finance committees we are often told, "We cannot treat people differently because we will offend the people who do not, or cannot, give." So in the end, churches send out one letter that may not offend those who do not give, but ignores and offends their most generous givers. Stop the insanity of treating everyone the same regarding form letters related to financial giving.

So what should the church leaders have done? How could they have communicated the need while at the same time affirmed our friend and his generosity? Here are a few suggestions:

1. The letter should have been personalized, not a form letter.
2. The first words of the letter should have been "Thank you for your generous giving."
3. The next sentence should have shared about a ministry in the church and how it has affected people's lives in a positive way.
4. After a thank-you and a ministry story, there could then be a request to prayerfully consider making a gift over and above the individual's regular giving in order to continue a particularly important ministry.

Insanity: Offertory Performance

Even though the congregation may expect a musical performance, or a five-minute solo by the organist or pianist, why not allow a five-minute word of witness from someone whose life has been changed because of the church's ministry? What about an opportunity for groups or individuals to say thank you for a particular ministry? Other nonprofits would die for the opportunity to have all their donors in one place every week, both to tell their story and to say thank you. Do not waste an opportunity to say thank you just because there has always been a musical interlude during the offering. Instead, come up with at least one story of transformation a month, or one person or group that wants to say thank you for donations to their particular ministry.

Here are a few suggestions:

1. Invite people to speak during this time and make sure they adhere to the five-minute time limit.

2. Make sure this is an opportunity for people to say thank you and relate the impact that a church ministry has had on them.

3. This should not be an opportunity to ask for more donations. This is simply an opportunity to say thank you.

4. Be creative! Use video clips of children, youth, or shut-ins saying thank you to the congregation.

5. Take time during staff meetings to brainstorm about people who would be an effective witness or have a powerful story to share.

Insanity: Excessive Debt

One of the benefits of our current economic downturn has been our heightened sensitivity to debt. People appear to be increasingly aware of the negative consequences of excessive debt, whether government, personal, or church debt. Unfortunately, many of our churches already carry burdens of overwhelming debt. We routinely see churches that pay up to 40 percent of their operating budget toward debt.

When 30 to 40 percent of a church's operational budget goes to pay off debt, the congregation is discouraged and new ministry is hindered. For example, a pastor recently poured out her frustration with a budget that had 40 percent of income going toward debt payments. The church was growing, but new members were reluctant to step up their giving. Why? They didn't want forty cents of every dollar they gave going to pay off debt, especially long-term debt with no end in sight. Major donors to any organization, according to Panas, want "confidence that the organization will use [their] money wisely."[3] Most givers will not equate excessive debt with using one's money wisely!

What constitutes excessive debt? In our experience, 10 to 12 percent of operating income is a healthy debt level for most churches and is easily managed. Debt levels of 13 to 16 percent are somewhat manageable but could affect ministry and staff. Debt levels of 17 to 20 percent will most certainly affect ministry but can be sustainable for the short term. Churches should proceed with caution at this level of debt. Any debt over 20 percent places most churches in jeopardy of being unable to sustain the programs and staff needed to be viable and growing. Here is another way to consider what constitutes excessive debt. If your project requires you to conduct more than two consecutive capital campaigns before you can incorporate the debt into your budget, it may be too costly.

In our discussions with churches carrying more than 20 percent debt, we have heard how they succumbed to the allure of the "Field of Dreams" theory of church growth: "Build it, and they will come." This might have worked in a late '80s movie, set in an Iowa cornfield, but it won't work for most churches. Build it, and they might visit. But unless strong ministries and programs are in place, visitors will not stay, and they will not give.

So what do churches do when they discover their debt load hinders giving, growth, ministry, and mission? Most important, these churches need to have a strategy. We are continually amazed at how many churches with excessive debt have no plan in place to resolve the debt other than car washes and bake sales. The most successful strategy for dealing with excessive debt is to keep interest payments as part of the operating budget and then conduct a capital campaign with all monies going to principal reduction. People respond favorably to actually seeing progress in paying down the principal.

Insanity: Adults Only

Every stewardship campaign should have a component for teaching and encouraging children and youth in their giving. It is surprising when church leaders say, "Surely we cannot ask our children and youth to give." If we believe we are blessed when we give, why would we deny our children the opportunity to experience the joys and blessings of giving? If we do not teach our children about giving and tithing, why do we think that somehow as adults they will begin to give or tithe? Any time we speak with adults about giving and generosity, there should be a lesson for our children and youth. Dave Ramsey, a nationally known speaker on personal finances, said this when asked about children and tithing:

> God tells us to tithe, but it's not a sin or salvation issue. It's because it's good for us to learn to become givers. When you're a giver, you're more Christ-like. I wouldn't require a child to give, but I would help them to understand early and often to be a giver. As our kids grew up, we always had them give some, save some, and spend some, but I never wanted them to do it as a rule. It's to teach them the character and qualities of being a giver.[4]

Many churches will give Bibles to children at a certain age. Why not pick another age at which to give children a giving bank with three separate components: spending, saving, and giving? Included with the banks would be instructions and suggestions for parents to help guide their children in giving. Maybe the parents will be encouraged to step up their own giving! There are many sources and suggestions on the Internet for including children and youth in giving. One of the best ways to strengthen the financial future of the church is through teaching our children and young people the joys of giving. Stop the insanity of adult-only stewardship.[5]

Stop the Insanity: To-Do List

1. Stop printing financial numbers in the bulletin every week.
2. Stop dividing your budget by fifty-two or twelve to determine how much you need per week or month. Instead, use a five-year average for a given month or time frame.
3. Stop sending out the same letters to everyone, givers and nongivers alike.
4. Every letter sent to a giver should begin with his or her name and a thank-you.
5. At least once a month, use the offertory as a time for personal witness from someone whose life has been affected by a ministry of the church.
6. If your church has debt, take the time to determine what percentage of your budget goes to debt payments. If it's above 20 percent, get help and put a plan in place now to reduce that percentage.
7. Give banks, not just Bibles, to children.
8. Teach children and youth about giving and generosity.
9. Consider providing commitment cards to children and youth and inviting them to share their giving stories with the congregation.

THANK.
ASK.
REPEAT.

Saying thank you is more than good manners. It is good spirituality.
Alfred Painter

Creating a cycle of thanking and asking is key to increasing giving in your church. According to Giving USA, from 1987 to 2011, giving to religious organizations as a percentage of total charitable giving declined from 52 to 32 percent.[1] The total amount of contributions to both churches and other religious charities is plummeting rapidly. There is no question that the significant decrease in giving to churches is due to nonprofits doing a better job of thanking and asking. Saying thank you is a critical component of your stewardship efforts and allows you to model gratitude to the congregation. Thanking those who support your ministry strengthens partnerships and paves the way for opportunities to ask for additional gifts in the future. In fact, if you have not said, "Thank you," you have no business asking for another gift. Once you have gotten into this rhythm of thanking and asking, it will become a natural part of your year-round stewardship efforts, and giving will increase.

Many times donors are asked to repeat their gift before they are thanked for their first gift. Have you ever made a donation and wondered if it was received? Have you ever contributed to an organization and never heard from it again? If you belong to any church in America, the answer is probably yes! Remember that other nonprofits are working diligently to woo your donors, and statistics indicate they are succeeding. Thank those who pledge and contribute to your annual operating budget. As soon as pledges are received, send an acknowledgement of the pledge by your financial secretary in a thank-you note. At the same time, your governing body should write personal thank-you notes to each household that has made a pledge. In addition, the top 10 percent of pledgers should receive a personal note from the pastor. First-time pledgers and those whose pledges increased substantially should also receive a note from the pastor. At the least, thank-you notes for plate donations and pledge gifts should be sent to donors quarterly. The purposes of these notes are to 1) express gratitude for the contribution and 2) reduce "buyer's remorse" or any ambiguity by letting donors know how their investments will be used for ministry. For example:

> Dear Joe and Mary,
>
> Thank you so much for your recent pledge in support of the ministries of St. Swithin's Church. As a member of the leadership council, I want you to know how much we appreciate the generous support you and others in our parish provide. As a result of the 20 percent increase in pledges this year, we will be able to move Jim, our associate pastor, from part-time to a full-time position. He is eager to begin working more closely with our youth and small group ministry programs.

Blessings to you and thank you for partnering with St. Swithins in fulfilling God's vision for our ministry.

In addition, you have an opportunity to thank donors on giving statements and let them know how you will be putting their gifts to good use in the future. For example:

Thank you for your contributions in support of the ministry of First Church. In the first quarter, thanks to the generosity of our members, we were able to provide scholarships to six of our youth for their alternative spring break. As one of them remarked, "Being able to work on the Habitat Project helped me to see how lucky I am. It was great to get to know the family!" With the continual support of our members, we plan to enhance our website to promote better church communication. Thank you for partnering with us in this ministry.

These notes let your donors know their support is appreciated and tells them what you will do with their donations. Thank-you notes should also be written to those who provide financial (outside the budget) and volunteer support. Committee chairs, staff, and other church leaders will encourage a culture of gratitude by regularly thanking those who support specific areas of ministry. In one church, a member realized her annual pledge was contributing close to 10 percent of the church's annual budget. She was concerned that increasing her pledge might put the church in jeopardy if she should move or die; however, she wanted to do more. The church needed to upgrade its computer equipment in order to increase efficiency and improve church-wide communication. After several inquiries, she was told a gift of $5,000 would accomplish the task. One year after making the gift to her church, she still had received no acknowledgement of the gift or explanation of how the money had been spent. During this same time, one of her favorite charities had sent a thank-you note after each of the four donations she had made. The most recent donation had elicited a phone call from the executive director simply to say thank you. When this donor considers future philanthropic options, which organization do you suppose she will choose?

Once you have established a culture of gratitude and expressing thanks, you will be in a position to ask donors for their support in multiple ways. Keep in mind that asking a donor to support your ministry is not about pressure or coercion. It is about inviting them to return to God a portion of the blessings they have received. It is about asking them to partner in significant ministries that are transformational and help fulfill God's vision. The "ask" makes it possible for your church to feed the hungry, clothe the naked, and heal the sick. This is holy, sacred, Kingdom-building work!

Most likely, you are already asking for annual pledges and contributions to support your ongoing ministry needs, but there are several other opportunities for engaging members and increasing giving to the church. Capital needs and legacy gifts for long-term investments are additional "ask" opportunities.

Annual Pledges

Most churches continue to use pledge cards, typically mailed to and returned by members indicating their intentions for a yearly donation. While pledge cards are still useful, it is important to consider how you are using them to communicate giving opportunities. For example, if someone joins your congregation in December, will he or she be given a pledge card, or will it wait until the fall appeal? Do you mail out your pledge cards in hopes they will somehow find their way back to the church? Do you follow up with those who have not returned a pledge card to let them know their support of your ministries is important?

One of the most effective changes you can make in terms of the annual appeal is to alter the way pledge cards are presented. Instead of mailing pledge cards in advance, let members know everyone will complete pledge cards together in worship, as a faithful community. During worship, allow time for pledge cards to be completed, and invite people to come forward and offer their pledges to the church on the altar. This symbolic but powerful expression of sacrifice conveys volumes about the spiritual aspects of making a pledge. For those who are not in worship on pledge-card Sunday, mail a pledge card immediately to them, letting them know how important their participation is to the ministry of your church. One week later, have your governing body make contact with those who have not yet returned a pledge card. The immediacy of your contacts will convey the importance of their partnership in ministry. Remember, this is not about encouraging people to fund your budget. This is about inviting people to return to God a portion of blessings that will enable your church to do Kingdom building. Make sure those who join your church between annual appeals are given the opportunity to partner with you in ministry. A one-on-one conversation with clergy or a lay leader is most effective.

Capital Gifts

At any given moment, the pastor should be prepared with a list of ten capital projects or purchases that would assist the church in fulfilling its vision. The cost of these projects/purchases could be relatively small ($5,000 to $20,000) or large (greater than the annual budget). The projects should be ready and waiting for nothing but the funds with which to execute them. The list should be posted on the church's website and frequently communicated in church media. The projects list should include a description of the project and its cost. Most important, the list should include a description of who will be affected by the completion of the project. In other words, what ministry will this project enable, and who will benefit?

Most churches have families with resources to give more than their annual contributions. Occasionally, these families will inquire about additional giving opportunities, but it is important to be proactive and *ask* for their support. Members who have consistently given substantial support to the annual budget, who are engaged in the ministries of your church, and who have additional resources are your most likely contributors. Assuming you have already established a culture of expressing thanks, these donors will already be in regular communication with the pastor or other lay leaders. A simple phone call to say, "I would like to stop by and share some ideas for growing the music ministry" should suffice. Once there, invite the donor's advice on the proposed project. Get some insight as to whether this project resonates with her or his philanthropic goals before asking for the gift. Donors of this nature are typically savvy and understand you may be soliciting their support. Even if the project does not appeal to the individual, you have still accomplished a great deal. Your donor will feel a closer partnership with your ministry and affirmation because you have asked for his or her advice. In turn, the individual will be eager to find a project that more closely aligns with his or her interests. If the donor chooses to support your project, you will have forged a closer connection and cultivated a strong partner in ministry.

Legacy Gifts

The most important stewardship ministry in which you will be engaged is the cultivation of legacy or planned gifts. Donors who make legacy gifts to your church from their estates, 401K plans, life insurance policies, or gift annuities have given you the most special gift imaginable. Legacy gifts result when someone identifies your church as a beneficiary of assets received upon the death of the donor. These assets represent the accumulation of wealth over a lifetime. By providing for your church in his or her will, the donor has expressed ultimate trust that the funds will be used as the donor wishes. Asking for and accepting legacy gifts is a huge responsibility, not to be taken lightly. If you have any doubt that the proposed gift might not be used as specified in the distribution of the donor's estate, the gift must be declined rather than used inappropriately. Legacy donors do not have to be what most would consider "wealthy." Anyone can make a legacy gift to the church. Typically, legacy gift candidates are people who have consistently supported the church's annual budget for at least five years. These members have demonstrated a desire to be in relationship with the church and may be willing to support the church in perpetuity. There are several potential planned-giving vehicles that can be considered, but by far the most common is the bequest. A gift provided for in a will or estate plan, bequests can be written in a variety of ways at the discretion of the donor, including the following:

1. A specific dollar amount
2. A percentage of the entire estate
3. Either of the above, contingent upon the death of spouse or dependents

Gifts can be specified for a particular purpose or given without restrictions. A gift acceptance policy is vital to ensuring you have predetermined the restrictions with which you are willing to comply and those you may want to avoid. Keep in mind that a gift received without restrictions simplifies the administrative process, but ultimately the donor will decide whether a gift is made with restrictions. Understanding the donor's wishes in advance of death is extremely helpful both in honoring the donor's intent and in setting an example that others will be keen to see. Suppose that Betty, a member of your congregation, is considering putting the church in her will for $500,000. She hopes her gift will create an endowment fund for youth ministry and fund scholarships for youth to attend the denominational summer camp. Recently, a fellow church member and friend of Betty's passed away, leaving $100,000 to the church with the restriction that it be used for the music program. Betty watches as the church staff and lay leadership argue over how best to use this gift. Ultimately, the gift is used by the church to balance the budget and pave the parking lot. At the same time, a representative from Betty's university visits her and asks if she would like to endow a chair at her college. Her university has a long and rich history of celebrating those whose legacies live on through the various colleges. Where do you think Betty chose to leave a legacy? This scenario plays out every day in churches.

By asking a donor for a legacy gift, you tell the donor you understand how important the church is in her life. You are saying, "We know how important First Church has always been to you. Your ongoing support of our ministries will make a difference in the lives of our children, grandchildren, and those who come after them. You can trust that your gift will be the legacy of your lifetime." Asking for a legacy gift is a great responsibility. Receiving one is a huge honor.

Now, you have thanked your donors and asked them for continual support of your various ministries, but have you made giving easy? Keeping in mind the diversity of generations represented in most churches, you will want to consider multiple vehicles through which members can make donations to your church. For example, every church should make use of pledges, online donations (EFT [electronic funds transfer] and through your website), and weekly loose plate offerings. You may also want to consider giving kiosks, QR codes, and smartphone giving. Giving kiosks typically resemble ATMs, although the latest versions make use of iPad technology and are more streamlined. Programs can be added to your giving kiosk to allow people to register for programs, sign up for events, and become more involved in your ministry. QR codes can be used to drive people to your website to view a video or other materials. Once on your website, your "donate here" or similar button can move people to an online donation. Church apps are also popping up that allow donors to make a gift to the church directly from their cell phones. This is particularly helpful because people are carrying less cash. Special appeals from the pulpit may garner significant emotional support, but if the only vehicle for contributing is cash, it may fall short. According to the Lake Institute on Faith and Giving, "There is a decided change in giving patterns. Church envelopes have long been the preferred way of giving but this practice is fading fast. Automatic banking, credit cards, church giving kiosks and numerous forms of online giving challenge congregations to rethink their fundraising practices."[2] Even relatively small congregations can implement these options, which will eventually become the norm rather than the exception.

Thank. Ask. Repeat: To-Do List

1. Establish a system for acknowledging pledges as they are received.

2. Organize your governing body to write thank-you notes to pledging households; remember, your pastor should write thank-you notes to the top 10 percent of pledgers, those who have increased their pledge substantially, and new pledgers. Provide an example letter from which they are to write letters.

3. Work with the church office to determine timing of giving statements (hopefully, you are sending them out at least quarterly). Include a thank-you note in statements and let people know how funds were spent. Let people know your ministry needs for the next few months.

4. Plan to distribute and collect pledges in worship as a part of your worship service.

5. Develop a list of ten capital projects or purchases that would help further your ministry objectives. Write a description of each project including cost, timing, and who will be affected. Make a list of those in your church who have been financially supportive and may have the resources to fund one or more items on the list.

6. Develop a program to promote your legacy giving program. Include information about how to name the church in a will or estate. When a legacy gift is received, be sure to express gratitude to the donor publicly and let people know the funds were used for purposes specified by the donor.

7. Research giving opportunities beyond the pledge and offering plate. If you have not included online giving as an option yet, now is the time to get started. Discuss

other options for giving that might work for your congregation, keeping in mind your target audience may include people of different ages with church experiences that differ from yours. Many of these options are fairly low cost and will quickly pay for themselves with increased giving.

Chapter Seven

GIVE A WORD
OF WITNESS

Illness stole my song . . . now I sing for you.
I was depressed and anorexic . . . now I'm joyful and happy.
Once lukewarm and indifferent to God . . .
today on fire in serving God.
Lost our fourteen-year-old son . . . surviving
on your prayers and hugs.

One of the most powerful tools for growing generosity in the church is telling the story of how the church is transforming people's lives through its ministry. Every church has (or should have) an abundance of people who can provide witness to the ways in which their lives have been positively impacted by the people, programs, and ministries of the church. In many cases, churches continue to plug along without sharing their stories, and eventually these churches come to believe they have no story to tell.

For example, in one United Methodist Church, the capital campaign was building momentum and reaching its peak as we were closing in on Pledge Sunday. The campaign raised funds to eliminate the remaining debt from building a youth and discipleship building. Up to this point, the campaign was garnering significant support. Then, during the final meeting of the campaign leadership, the pastor dropped a bombshell and said he had just heard from the bishop that he was being transferred to another congregation. Stunned, disappointed, and discouraged, the leadership talked about what to do and how to inform the congregation about the loss of their beloved pastor.

As the leadership committee prayed and talked about what to do next, the youth pastor quietly suggested we watch a five-minute video he had brought to share. As the video began to play, a beautiful teenage girl came on the screen. The first words out of her mouth were, "My first memory as a child is seeing my father attempt to kill my mother." She had our attention. She continued to talk about how, just as her mother had finally gotten the courage to leave her abusive father, the church they were attending kicked them out. At a very young age, she had been taught she was unworthy of any real love. She had allowed herself to be used and abused. In a calm but steady voice, she spoke of once believing she had nothing to live for, no reason to go on. But then something changed. When she came to the youth group at the church, she was noticed and treated with love and respect for the first time in her life. Then she turned to the camera and said, "Thank you for being the church. Thank you for loving me. You saved my life." There wasn't a dry eye in the house. The campaign leaders left the meeting with a renewed sense of purpose and determination. And in the end, even with the well-loved pastor leaving, the capital campaign was amazingly successful.

In many of the churches in which we work, church members and clergy are reluctant to tell stories like this. Some will say, "It makes us feel uncomfortable. Aren't we just manipulating people emotionally?" Behind these comments lies a fear—

not of being uncomfortable with the stories, but that maybe their church doesn't have anyone with this kind of witness. The worry is, "What if we don't have anyone whose life has been changed by the power of the gospel?" If you truly don't have anyone whose life has been affected by the ministries of your church, it is probably time to reassess the purposes and effectiveness of the church. Every church has people whose lives have been forever changed by the power of God through Jesus Christ. We donate in order to make a difference in other people's lives. If you want to increase giving to support your ministries, help people see how lives are being changed through their generosity. Tell stories not about the budget or bricks, but about the impact your ministries are having on the lives of those you serve. People want to know their giving is making a difference in the life of another—give a word of witness!

One of the first challenges is in the identification of people who have a story to tell. Clergy and lay leaders will often say, "But we don't have people like that." Really? So there haven't been any youth whose lives have been changed by your youth program? Nobody in your church has struggled with depression and come back into light and hope? No one in the church has moved through the process of grief to new life and peace? No couples have been praying for a child and now find themselves to be proud parents? No one has been diagnosed with cancer and is now in remission? Everyone has a story to share. The question is simple: Is my life different because of my relationship with God and this church?

One church had a Mechanics Ministry team that repaired used cars and donated them to people in the community who did not have transportation. One Sunday, a single mother with four small children told her story to the congregation. She said she just wanted to thank the church for giving her back her dignity and self-respect. At some point after her car had crossed over the 250,000-mile mark, it had stopped running altogether. As a result, she had been unable to keep a job and care for her family. Government assistance made it possible to feed her family, assuming she could find a ride to the grocery store. Since receiving her car from the Mechanics Ministry, she said she was able to get a good-paying job, drive her children to school, and become self-sufficient. She said that this church had shown her God's love and compassion when she needed it the most. Can you imagine the offering collected that day on behalf of the Mechanics Ministry?

Telling stories of personal transformation can be done in a variety of ways. One way of sharing true stories of life before and after Christ can be done through "cardboard testimonies." Cardboard testimonies are a way to witness without having to say a word. A few words written on cardboard tell the before-and-after stories of the person holding the cardboard, conveying a powerful message. If you have never seen a cardboard testimony, search YouTube with the phrase "cardboard testimony" for examples. In short, a person writes a few words describing his old life on one side of the cardboard. On the other side, he writes a short description of his new life through Christ. For example, someone holds a cardboard sign that says "Addicted to alcohol." Then, the person flips the card over to reveal the words "Freed by grace." We've seen cardboard testimonies for everything from people giving witness to new life after cancer, to successful adoptions following a miscarriage, to hope following grief. In one of our churches, the beloved administrative assistant stood with a card that read, "Truck wrecks my car and breaks my body." Written on the other side was, "God sends me back to serve you and be loved back to health." In response, the entire congregation spontaneously stood in applause. Even in this older, very traditional mainline church, cardboard testimonies made an incredible impact. In fact, after the service, an eighty-five-year-old woman remarked through tear-filled eyes, "I've been coming to this church all my life and have never been so moved as I was this morning."

In a Catholic parish, the deacon was concerned that "cardboard testimonies did not sound very Catholic," but they chose to try them anyway. At all five masses, fifteen people shared their cardboard testimonies with the parish. Testimonies included everything from freedom from alcoholism to a couple who wrote about the loss of their son and how they were surviving on hugs and prayers from their church family. A fourteen-year-old youth with autism came up with a sign saying, "Bored in worship," with "Found the doughnut ministry" on the other side. At the end of every Mass, there was a standing ovation. Guess it ended up being Catholic after all.

Here is how to use cardboard testimonies as part of an annual stewardship campaign:

Recruit. One of the secrets to a successful cardboard testimony service is to recruit a diversity of people. The best cardboard testimonies include people of all ages and all walks of life. We have seen entire families do a cardboard testimony together. Ask people who are new to the church and people who have been members for fifty years. Remember, everyone has a story. As you begin to think about whom to recruit, start with a discussion in staff or church leadership meetings. After twenty to twenty-five individuals have been named, assign someone to ask them in person to participate. Assure them that you and others will assist them throughout the process. Ideally, you will have at least ten and as many as thirty cardboard testimonies at each service.

Train. While some of your recruits will know immediately what their cardboard testimonies will be, others will struggle and may become frustrated. Inviting those who are writing their cardboard testimonies to come together will alleviate some of the anxiety and actually help people refine what they want to write. At this meeting, the pastor should begin with a prayer. Then show a video from the many examples on YouTube. Try to find one that reflects your church's background and character. Pass out sheets of paper and pens and ask everyone to jot down ideas based on some of the following questions:

1. How has being a Christian changed your life?
2. What difference has coming to church made in your life?
3. How are you different now compared to how you were prior to church or knowing God?
4. How have you grown or changed over the years?
5. Name a time or event when God touched you in a profound or deep way.

During the meeting, have staff talk through people's stories with them and help them put their thoughts on paper. The biggest challenge will be reducing each story to five or six words per side of the board. Writing stories clearly but with as few words as possible is a crucial aspect of cardboard testimonies.

Practical Tips

To present the cardboard testimonies successfully, note the following tips:

1. Use white foam board that measures at least twenty by thirty inches. Finding and using actual cardboard cut from boxes can be extremely time consuming and is less

aesthetically pleasing. Use a large black chisel sharpie to write on the foam board.

2. Letters need to be at least four to six inches tall so they can easily be seen from any vantage point. You might choose to use stencils or draw light pencil lines on the foam board as a guide.

3. Get the entire group together for one rehearsal. Know where people will enter and where they will exit. Have them practice walking in holding the board for the count of five, flipping the board over, holding for a count of five, and then exiting the stage or platform. While one person walks off the stage, the next person should walk on. No words are spoken throughout the testimonies. Also, it is best to have people lined up in advance in the wings and ready to move across the front rather than have them come to the front from their pews or seats.

4. If possible, present live video of the cardboard testimonies as each individual walks out and shows his or her board.

5. Cardboard testimonies work best when the pastor agrees to participate, and he or she goes first, giving a brief explanation of cardboard testimonies beforehand.

At the conclusion of the cardboard testimonies, the pastor should share a five- to ten-minute message that ties together the cardboard testimonies and being moved to support the ministries of the church generously. The pastor may say something like the following:

This is what we are all about in this stewardship campaign. We are not just about dollars and cents, nor are we just about simply trying to meet the budget. This isn't about light bills and salaries. We are about changing lives with the power of God through Jesus Christ. Isn't this worthy of your investment?

Cardboard testimonies can be a powerful tool for telling a church's story of transforming lives, but they are not for everyone. You may need to consider other ways in which to invite members of the congregation to tell their personal stories of spiritual growth and transformation. Some churches have used a series of short videos featuring people who tell their own "before and after" stories. The benefit of video is that it can be edited to meet time and content restrictions. Video also can be distributed easily to a large number of people, by e-mailing a link or posting to your church's website, Facebook, or Twitter account. Regardless of the medium you choose, whether cardboard testimonies, videos, or in-person presentations, people want to know their giving makes a difference in people's lives. Find ways to tell stories about the real difference your church is making in people's lives, and you will cultivate bountiful generosity in the church.

Giving testimony about how God changes lives will encourage bountiful giving, but moving people to increase their giving substantially typically requires a slightly different type of witness. In talking with those who tithe or give above a 10 percent tithe, the most frequently named motivator is hearing the witness of a fellow church member. Hearing a respected friend or someone considered a peer talk about their giving is a highly effective way of moving people to bountiful giving.

Consider Sandy, who had belonged to her church for several years and never made a pledge. Routinely, she put her five dollars in the offering plate—at least during the weeks that she was in worship. To Sandy, five dollars seemed like a good contribution. After all, that was what her parents had always put in the plate when she attended church with them as a child. One Sunday, Sandy heard her pastor talk about giving and why she had become a tither. Sandy thought, "That's all well and good for the pastor. After all, she's the pastor, and besides, we give her a house, so she can afford to tithe." So once again, Sandy threw her five dollars in the plate.

The next Sunday, Sandy was surprised to see one of her friends nervously walk up to the pulpit. Sandy knew her friend's recent divorce had caused some financial challenges, and her friend sometimes struggled to pay her bills. Sandy listened carefully as her friend began to speak about all that God had done for her. She spoke about how the support of the church and her faith in God were the only things that got her through her divorce and her daughter's recent illness. Sandy went from being attentive to being flabbergasted when her friend next spoke about how she had been so blessed by God that she was moving toward being a tither. With joy on her face, her friend spoke about starting off by giving five dollars a week, just like Sandy. Then she spoke of her gratitude to God and how she wanted to give more in response. Five dollars became ten, and soon her friend was giving 5 percent of her teacher's salary back to God through their church. Her friend was now giving more than two thousand dollars a year to their church. But that wasn't the end. Her friend said that God had blessed her throughout her life, and she was going to increase her giving this year to 7½ percent of income. Next year, her plan was to tithe a full 10 percent to the church.

Sandy told the story of her friend's testimony years later, when she had become a successful business owner and a true tither. When we met her, Sandy was the largest contributor to her church. Sandy will tell anyone who will listen that her journey to bountiful generosity began the day she heard her friend talk about her giving and her friend's reasons for giving. The power of a layperson sharing a stewardship witness should never be underestimated. Provide opportunities for others to give a word of witness within the church regarding their tithe, in worship and in small groups, any time of the year, and experience bountiful generosity.

Telling your personal stewardship story takes some prayer, thought, and preparation. In chapter one, we spoke of stewardship as a journey grounded in gratitude, revealed in prayer, and lived in faith. These elements provide a helpful outline to a stewardship witness. For those who will share their journey, they should begin with gratitude. How have they been blessed by God and the church? Encourage them to be specific and personal, reaching beyond the most common expressions of gratitude for family, wealth, and health. Next, they should reflect in prayer, perhaps considering the questions "God, in light of all you have done for me, what would you have me do in return? God, what do you want me to give?" The most powerful stories are those that are honest about wrestling with God over gift amounts. Witnesses often include the struggles experienced when spouses have different opinions in regard to giving. The conclusion of the witness should include a response to God's will by stepping out in faith. How is a person's giving moving him or her out of a comfort zone and into a faith zone? Ultimately, the story with the most impact is the one that shares a personal experience of finding the will and the way to respond prayerfully and faithfully to God's leading.

As Mary and Bob stood in front of their congregation, they were obviously tense and uncomfortable. The pastor, having heard their story, had asked if they would be willing to share it in worship. After the usual introductory remarks, Mary quietly spoke of her battle with breast cancer. She thanked them for the prayer vigil held during her surgery as well as all the meals that had been prepared and delivered. Bob related how thankful he was for the men who had sat with him during the surgery and prayed with him while Mary was in recovery. Bob said,

Through you, God has blessed us immeasurably, far more than we could ever hope for. We believe Mary stands here because of God and you. When we first considered our gift to the capital campaign, we had settled on a gift of $5,000. We thought that was pretty good. Then we thought about whether or not our gift reflected our level of gratitude. Pretty soon the number was $10,000. Then we were asked to pray. Well, Mary likes to pray while walking the dog. Pretty soon the number was $20,000, and I told Mary I would walk the dog from now on. Now $20,000 may seem like a lot to you. It sure does to Mary and me, but we were still comfortable and knew we could manage that amount without any real problem. So then we heard about this thing called faith. Did our gift represent faith and sacrifice? We looked at each other and said almost simultaneously, "Okay, I guess now it's thirty." Thirty thousand will be a stretch. Making this gift will cause us to look at some of our vacation plans and put some of our remodeling plans on hold. But that's okay. What is a vacation or some new carpet compared to everything God has given us?

Thank you for being a part of our journey. Thirty thousand dollars may seem impossibly high for you or it may seem too small. The amount isn't important. It's all about the journey. Join us please in the journey of gratitude, prayer, and faith. We love you. Thank you.

As Bob and Mary returned to their pew, eyes glistening with tears, the entire congregation stood as one and gave a resounding, "AMEN!"

Whether in person or through video, a personal challenge

from a respected friend and peer will do more for increasing bountiful generosity than any sermon. As with cardboard testimonies, one of the keys is in the recruiting. Don't just default to the usual people who have stood in front of the congregation year after year. Ask people who may be a surprise, people like Bob and Mary with a story to tell. Bob and Mary were selected after the pastor looked at the giving records and realized this relatively new family had already made a significant financial investment in the church's ministries. Recruit a young family who is just starting out with a new home but giving a percentage of income that exceeds your average donation. Recruit the person on the "fixed income" who continues to give generously. Some of the most effective stewardship witnesses have been older children or teens who have made a commitment to give substantially, even tithe, at a young age.

Once you have recruited people to give their stewardship witnesses, review your expectations for their time of sharing with the congregation or small group:

Length. A stewardship witness should last five to seven minutes. The content should include highlights of gratitude, prayer, and faith. Provide a copy of Bob and Mary's remarks to your stewardship witnesses, as an example to follow.

Content. Encourage those who will share their witness to be detailed and specific about their giving and the events that led them to give at their current level. Bob and Mary talked specific amounts. While some people were uncomfortable, it reminds people that this is serious business and not to be taken lightly. It raises expectations and helps people realize the magnitude of sacrifice being made by those giving witness. If people are unwilling to share specific amounts, ask them to share percentages or give examples such as giving the equivalent of a car payment or a vacation or home remodeling project. This communicates the depth of faith and commitment to which they are witnessing. When talking about annual giving, use percentages and moving up toward or beyond tithing. Always end with an encouragement and challenge for people to join you on the journey.

Write it down. People who prepare their remarks in advance are less likely to exceed the time limit. It will also be beneficial for the pastor to review the remarks before they are made in worship.

Give a Word of Witness: To-Do List

1. Begin having discussions at every staff and church leadership meeting about people who have had their lives touched and changed in significant ways. This will give you a list of names to draw from as you choose stewardship witnesses.

2. Have the pastor review the giving list to identify people or families who have clearly stepped up in their giving. Schedule a visit and find out why.

3. Schedule at least one stewardship witness per month, in person or by video. Do not do stewardship witnesses only during the annual campaign. People may be "programmed" at that time to tune out.

4. Once a year, have a real celebration of lives transformed. Use cardboard testimonies or multiple video clips.

5. Be intentional about recruiting a diverse group of people for the testimonies—people who represent various age groups, lengths of membership, races, levels of socioeconomic status, and so forth.

Chapter Eight

ASK THE RIGHT QUESTION

*A small body of determined spirits fired by an
unquenchable faith in their mission
can alter the course of history.*
Mahatma Gandhi

We wrote this book to address the most pressing question in the minds of most church leaders we encounter today: "How can we raise more money?" Initially, we planned to offer tools that could be implemented immediately into stewardship efforts for quick results. However, while working with churches and nonprofits, we have come to believe that "how can we raise more money?" is the wrong question. Instead of asking *how*, church leaders should be asking *why*. Because of the economic downturn and subsequent decrease in giving and attendance in the mainline church, most church leaders fear not having enough resources. Coupled with the nonprofits that take a piece of the charitable pie once enjoyed by churches, the need to raise additional financial resources is significant in most churches. Instead of focusing on "How can we raise more money?" church leaders should take a step back and ask the most important money-raising question of all: "Why would someone want to support our ministry?"

In the midst of conducting one capital campaign, we were invited to attend the operating-budget discussion held by the church's governing board. Twenty Christians sitting around tables were having a heated discussion about what staff should be cut and what programs or ministries should be eliminated. Keep in mind, this church was in the process of conducting a capital campaign for much-needed repairs and improvements to church infrastructure. Of course, everyone present, including the staff, had his or her own agenda. At one point in the debate, a church member asked, "If we were a business and experiencing this kind of decline or stagnation, wouldn't we just close the doors? If not close the doors, we certainly wouldn't be thinking about making additional capital expenditures to our building!" One of the church leaders, who up to this point had been quiet, said,

> I guess it depends on whether or not we believe we have a worthwhile product. If we have something we believe is needed by people and will make a difference in their lives, then we should not close our doors but do everything possible to continue getting our "product" out to people. I guess it depends on whether or not we think our church is offering anything worthwhile to our community and the world. And if the people around this table don't think we have the answer to a world that is broken and hurting we probably should put a "for sale" sign on the front door right now.

Before the Hershey Half-Marathon, an e-mail was sent to participants by race coordinators with an attached link to their Runner's Guide, which included the banner headline "Why Runners Run." Following the headline were pictures of children who had been cared for at Hershey Medical Center, including premature babies in incubators and young children fighting cancer. The Runner's Guide also shared the story of Corbin, a young boy fighting a rare, life-threatening disease and, with the help of Hershey Medical Center, winning the battle. On race day, Corbin was introduced as the official starter. Furthermore, it was clear that proceeds from the race were going to the Children's Miracle Network to buy lifesaving equipment for the children's hospital at Hershey Medical Center. The headline and story were not about how much it cost to run the Hershey Medical Center. There was no mention of what the CEO was being paid or how much their utility bills were for the year. The focus was on a life being changed and how the runners were making a difference in a child's life.

According to the church newsletters and bulletins, if our churches were going to offer a Giver's Guide, the banner headline would probably read:

How to Keep Our Doors Open

or maybe:

How to Balance the Budget

If you want to increase giving and experience God's bounty, stop talking about budgets, bills, and survival, and start talking about mission, ministry, and changed lives. By focusing on the question *why* instead of *how*, ministries instead of budgets, and changed lives instead of paying bills, the mission and vision will be fulfilled. Every church needs to ask, "What business are we in, and why do we exist?" That is the question of mission.

Although churches may spend weeks and even months trying to come up with a mission statement, the truth is we already have been given our mission statement. We do not need a task force or study group to develop a mission statement. All we need to do is open our Bibles to Matthew 28:19–20:

> Go therefore and make disciples of all nations, baptizing them in the name of the Father and of the Son and of the Holy Spirit, and teaching them to obey everything that I have commanded you. And remember, I am with you always, to the end of the age.

The reason we exist as the church is simple. We exist to make disciples. And yet, if we are honest, we would admit that our actions often tell a very different story. We do not need a Bible study to determine the mission. We need reflection on and discussion of whether we really believe in our mission of making disciples. In churches of nearly every denomination across the country, we have asked, "When making a decision about a new program or ministry, what is the first question asked by the governing church body?" Almost unanimously, from churches of all persuasions, the answer is the same: "How much will it cost?" If our business is making disciples, shouldn't the determining question be "How is this going to help us accomplish our mission of making disciples?"

It has been said that it's not the church that has a mission, but God's mission that has a church." People give when they believe in the mission. If we believe a particular program or ministry will help us change people's lives, if we believe people will become disciples, don't we also believe God has the resources to make it happen?

So what is the question being asked in your church? Try taking a look at your church's most recent communication to the world with fresh eyes—by way of website, newsletter, or church bulletin. What are you communicating about your church's mission? Are you communicating "How can we raise more money?" Or are you demonstrating the transformational nature of your ministry?

Mission versus Vision

If you do not know where you are going,
every road will get you nowhere.
Henry Kissinger

The Great Commission to go forth and make disciples is the mission of every church. Then what is a church's vision? Our definition of *vision* is the specific way in which a church is being called to live out the mission in its community. How are you called to use your people and resources to make disciples for Christ? While the mission is the same for every church, each church has its own unique vision. For example, a posting on the *Christianity Today* website entitled "Popcorn in the Pews" describes a growing trend of churches that are holding worship in movie theaters. In 2003, National Cinemedia reported renting out 6 theaters to church groups. In 2009, the number of church rentals was 180. Churches holding worship in rented movie theaters share the same mission as a downtown cathedral with soaring spires, stained-glass windows, and pipe organs playing Bach and Beethoven. The "popcorn church" vision of how to accomplish the mission, however, is quite different.[1]

In order for a church to determine its unique vision, it must answer a few questions, including "Who are we called to reach?" and "What is the best way to reach them?" Most churches make the mistake of trying to appeal to everyone and end up appealing to very few. The popcorn church is trying to reach a very different demographic than the downtown cathedral is. How the popcorn church reaches its demographic is also unique—by including movie theater seating, popcorn, music, and theater ambience, which typically would not appeal to someone who has grown up in a high liturgy church setting. While these examples may be from opposite ends of the spectrum, they demonstrate the need for your church to identify who makes up your target demographic and how you will strategically plan to attract them.

Discovering God's Vision

Vision without execution is hallucination.
Thomas Edison

Discovering God's unique vision for your church requires intentional focus, study, and prayer. The first step in the process is to identify the needs of the community you serve. What are the demographics in your community? Is the community aging, or are families with young children moving in? Is the community struggling financially? Is the community growing or shrinking? What are other churches in the area providing? Is there a niche your church can fill? There are many resources available online as well as through the local Chamber of Commerce that can help with a demographics study of your community.

The discovery of your church's unique vision for ministry should also include a discussion of the passions of the congregation and church leadership. Consider, for example, a pastor who wrestles with the concept of vision for her church. Extensive reading on the topic of vision convinced her that the pastor should be the one to articulate the church's vision. She felt overwhelmed and had no idea where to begin. We asked her to consider the following questions:

- What do you really love about ministry?

- What are you passionate about in your day-to-day work?
- What keeps you getting up in the morning?

Furthermore, we suggested she consider the wisdom shared by theologian and writer Frederick Buechner, when he was asked, "What advice would you give a young person seeking a career?" Buechner's response was, "The vocation for you is the one in which your deep gladness and the world's deep need meet. . . . Something that not only makes you happy but that the world needs to have done."[2]

Articulating the church's vision begins with uncovering or re-discovering the pastor's passion for ministry and inviting your congregation to discover theirs. The church's vision for ministry will be found at the confluence of pastoral and congregational passions.

This pastor began to talk about her call to ministry, which was rooted in Matthew 25:35–36:

> For I was hungry and you gave me food, I was thirsty and you gave me something to drink, I was a stranger and you welcomed me, I was naked and you gave me clothing, I was sick and you took care of me, I was in prison and you visited me.

She felt most alive when involved in her church's many ministries to the "least of these" in her downtown area. As she told of the lives that had been changed by her church's downtown ministry, her voice and demeanor became alive and energized. She was passionate about urban ministry!

Like many of our churches, her church was struggling with declining attendance, diminishing finances, and an urgent need for capital repairs on a beautiful, old building. Her church was home to, among other ministries, a food pantry that helped hundreds of people a month, as well as a computer room dedicated to a program for inner-city kids in need of after-school care and tutoring. One of the former food pantry clients, Jim, had become a church member and now assisted in the food pantry, unloading trucks and bagging food. While Jim doesn't have an official residence, he says he found his real home at the church. This church was deeply engaged in urban ministry—a shared passion of the church leadership and the congregation.

The intersecting point of the passions shared by the congregation and the church leadership now becomes the beginning of the church's unique vision. Taking liberties with Frederick Buechner's statement and applying it directly to churches and vision, we might say:

> *Vision is the place where the shared passions of church leadership and congregation intersect with a great need of your community.*

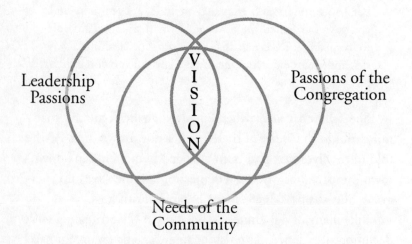

So what is the difference between any other nonprofit and the church? Couldn't this also apply to the United Way, Red Cross, homeless shelters, and a myriad of other worthy causes? There are two significant differences:

1. Always remember the mission. In the end, the mission is what separates the church from other nonprofits. The vision is how we are called by God to live out our mission in our particular community.

2. Vision must always be discerned through prayer. Vision is never about simply using the latest business strategy and applying it to the church. Planning retreats need to be supported by prayer retreats. In our experience, the greatest asset we have in the church, the Spirit of God, is often neglected or ignored in favor of the latest and newest corporate model for strategic planning. Vision begins and ends with prayer.

As you seek to discern God's unique vision for your church, begin by having your pastor and staff ask questions found earlier in the chapter:

- What do you really love about ministry?
- What are you passionate about in your day-to-day work?
- What keeps you getting up in the morning?

Second, develop a systemic plan for listening to individuals and groups within the church. This may be a combination of one-on-one meetings or group meetings. The agenda for these meetings is the same—discover a common passion for ministry. Even with as many as five hundred people present, there are often common themes and passions that rise to the surface. Before and during these meetings, it is important to lay a foundation of prayer. A prayer vigil before as well as prayer support during the meetings will always be beneficial. Questions to be considered for vision discernment meetings include the following:

- Why did you join our church, and why do you stay?
- What ministries are you passionate about?
- What do we do better than anyone else does?
- What do you see as a primary need of our community?
- If our church were given a million dollars, what would you do with it?
- Why would someone want to support our ministry?

As you gather this information, look for points of intersection where shared passion and community needs meet.

A word of warning: a specific vision for ministry may create conflict and tension with some members. Consider Jim, the homeless man who now is a regular worship attender. In some churches, Jim's presence might cause some members to express discomfort or be upset about having a homeless person in the church. A few members might become disgruntled over "having all those kids" in church. A clear and specific vision may give rise to a bit of conflict and tension, but it will also lead to vibrant ministry and financial bounty.

Experiencing the bounty of generous giving begins with asking the right question: "Why?" Why would people want to support our ministry, especially when there are so many other worthy organizations? Your church has the answer to a broken and hurting world. Your church is called by the Great Commission to share the good news! Your unique vision will enable you to clearly and convincingly engage your members in bountiful, generous giving.

Ask the Right Question: To-Do List

1. At every council or leadership meeting, have some kind of a symbol to remind you of God's presence. This will remind you to focus on God's mission for your church rather than anyone's personal agenda. A lit candle in the center of the table or offering Communion during your meetings will help everyone present to stay focused on God's will.

2. Ask someone who does not attend your church to look at your website and read your newsletter and bulletin while asking the following questions:

   What drives this church?
   What seems to be most important to this church?
   What business is this church in?

3. Set up interviews with your top twenty givers and ask some of the following questions:

   What do you love most about your church?
   What ministry are you passionate about in our church?
   What sets us apart from other churches?
   If we had a million-dollar gift given to the church, where would you spend it?

4. Conduct a series of home gatherings and ask the same questions listed above.

5. Have staff or a small group of leaders look at all programs and ministries and ask, "Is there anything that really sets us apart from other churches?" This may

help you identify whom you are reaching and how you should be reaching them.

6. Purchase or utilize denominational demographic material to begin looking at the makeup of the community you serve and identifying specific potential needs.

7. Talk to school principals, superintendents, local politicians, the chief of police, and other community leaders to learn more about what needs remain unfulfilled.

8. Conduct a leadership retreat and go over all of the information gleaned from items 1–7. Be sure to include a prayer vigil and other time for touching base with God.

Chapter Nine

MAKE STEWARDSHIP YEAR ROUND

There is a time for everything,
and a season for every activity under heaven.
Ecclesiastes 3:1 (NIV)

Most churches agree that stewardship should not be limited to the fall's annual stewardship campaign but rather warrants a year-round emphasis. In our experience, however, most churches fail to make stewardship a priority any time other than during their fall appeal. Once the annual stewardship process is completed, most stewardship committees go into hibernation until someone rallies them together the following summer. In order to experience bountiful giving and generosity, don't limit focus on stewardship to the fall season or the annual pledge campaign. For hearts to change, teach and preach on stewardship the entire year.

Teach and Preach Stewardship

If you preach from the lectionary, there will be ample opportunity to preach on stewardship. As mentioned previously, eleven of Jesus' thirty-nine parables are devoted to the topic of money and possessions. Keep in mind the definition of stewardship as grounded in gratitude, revealed in prayer, lived in faith. Each step on this journey deserves its own focus and could be used to create a sermon and study series. Throughout the year, be sure to offer adult education opportunities on the topic of stewardship with materials such as DISCIPLE Bible Study or Crown Ministries. NOOMA videos are great conversation starters and are particularly effective with new and younger members. Some churches choose to focus on one particular area of stewardship per month. For example, January is environmental stewardship, February is stewardship of relationships, March is stewardship of the body, and so on. This particular approach is helpful in broadening people's understanding of stewardship beyond finances. People who are not typically receptive to the message of financial stewardship may be more easily engaged with this strategy. As mentioned in chapter five, be sure to include children in your stewardship teaching. Provide children with Bibles and banks as a great way to encourage their understanding of the theology of stewardship.

Year-Round Calendar

Here is a sample calendar demonstrating how you can make stewardship a priority year round:

Month	Activity
January	*Year-end statements.* Be sure to send a year-end statement to all who made a gift to your church (pledgers and nonpledgers). Obviously, this is needed for tax purposes, but it also provides an opportunity to say thank you to those who are supporting your ministry. Let them know how their gifts were put to good use. Let them know what you intend to do with their generous donations in the new year. *Annual meeting.* At the annual meeting of your congregation, the finance chair frequently is asked to present the line-item budget to the congregation and then ask for questions. Droning on about increasing healthcare costs and gas prices, the finance chair garners very little enthusiasm about bountiful giving! Is it any wonder these meetings are often poorly attended? You can still have the line-item budget available for those who want to see it (almost no one will), but try presenting a ministry-focused budget instead. Talk about your vibrant ministries and all the ways you are serving your community. Apportion your budget into ministry categories (worship, pastoral care, Christian education, communication, and outreach) based on the amount of resources spent in each area. For example, a clergyperson in a pastoral-size church may distribute costs related to her position as 50 percent worship (sermon preparation, working with musicians, etc.), 25 percent pastoral care (hospital visits, marriage counseling), 10 percent Christian education (adult education classes and confirmation), 10 percent communication (writing newsletters, visitor contacts), and 5 percent outreach (supporting food pantry, Kiwanis). Creating a ministry-focused budget is not an exact science, but your end result should reflect the amount of ministry that is being supported by the donations made by your members.

Month	Activity
February	*Stewardship committee.* Recruit new stewardship committee members and organize a retreat to plan for the year. Review the results of the fall stewardship process and consider how your process could be improved. During the retreat, be sure to include time for prayer, reflection, Bible study, and stewardship education. Open up conversations about money. Invite members to share their own stewardship experiences and where they are on their journeys. You may want to use this time to create a statement describing what your stewardship committee believes about giving and generosity. Include one stewardship witness in worship during February.
March	*New member class.* During the new member class, be sure to clearly articulate your church's vision for ministry and how you plan to accomplish it. Teach that stewardship is grounded in gratitude, revealed in prayer, and lived in faith. Provide an opportunity for new members to participate in giving through a pledge card, electronic giving, or other such means. You may want to offer prayer support for discernment on giving, such as a devotional book, stewardship prayers, or a list of Scriptures that relate to stewardship. Lent is a great time for prayer and reflection. Be sure your materials include the prayerful discernment of God's will for all resources. Include one stewardship witness in worship during March.

Month	Activity
April	*Quarterly statements.* Send quarterly statements that include a thank-you for gifts received and a description of what has been accomplished. Be sure to include information on what you intend to accomplish next with the gifts of your congregation. Present your wish list to the congregation. This is a list of projects or needs that fall outside the annual budget but are part of achieving your vision for ministry. Make sure you complete the "ask" by letting people know how much it will cost and to whom they should speak about making the gift. Include one stewardship witness in worship during April.
May	*Planned giving.* Host a workshop on estates and wills and invite the entire congregation. Although the average age for a person creating his or her first will is forty, most people in the United States die without a will or estate plan. Invite a local expert to encourage people to create a simple will. Also, be sure to provide language that enables people to include your church in their will easily, as either sole beneficiary, partial beneficiary (dollar amount or percentage), or beneficiary contingent on the death of other heirs. If you don't already have one, establish an endowment fund. We recommend you create an endowment fund with a specified purpose before receiving a large gift, rather than after, when it is likely to cause some conflict. Begin a new tradition of providing fourth graders with banks divided into three sections: Save/Spend/Share (available from various resources online). Include one stewardship witness in worship during May.

Month	Activity
June	*Time and talent.* This is a great time to identify new leadership in preparation for fall programming. Host an adult forum on spiritual gifts, possibly including a spiritual gifts inventory. Prepare a list of ministry areas within the church along with current leadership of those areas and their contact information. Ask members to consider how they may use their spiritual gifts in support of the ministries of your church. You may wish to have them complete a pledge card indicating their areas of interest. If someone completes a card and indicates interest, it is vitally important that he or she is asked to serve. So often, time and talent surveys are taken but volunteers are never called to serve. Include one stewardship witness in worship during June.
July	*Quarterly statements.* Send quarterly statements and be sure that thank-you notes are written and sent as well; now is also a good time to send thank-you notes to those who have been involved in leadership or served the church in significant ways. *Online and electronic giving.* Review your processes for online and electronic giving through EFT (electronic funds transfer). Test it out and be sure it is user friendly and convenient. Promote this opportunity to the congregation, providing testimony from those who are giving electronically. Include one stewardship witness in worship during July.

Month	Activity
August	*Communication materials.* Review your communication materials and ask, What do they say to an outsider about our church's priorities? Do they say, "Our costs are up and we need more money," or do they say, "We are a thriving community going about building God's kingdom—come and join us!" Review church newsletters, bulletins, the church website, and other communications to be sure they reflect gratitude and abundance. Include one stewardship witness in worship during August.
September	*New member class.* Include one stewardship witness in worship during September.
October	*Send quarterly statements.* This will be timed so that members are reminded of the amount of their pledges just prior to the launch of the annual financial appeal. Financial stewardship process—seven weeks: *First Sunday.* Pastor shares stewardship witness. Distribute devotional guide to congregation and invite them to be in prayer. *Second Sunday.* Gratitude Sunday. Pastor preaches on God as the source of all gifts; distribute index cards that say, "I am grateful to God for _____," and ask people to complete the cards in worship. Following Sunday Two/Gratitude Sunday, display gratitude cards in a high-traffic area so people will see them throughout the week. Include a lay-stewardship witness in worship. *Third Sunday.* Cardboard testimonies. Have members share their witness through cardboard testimonies during worship.

Month	Activity
November	*Fourth Sunday.* Commitment Sunday. Pledge cards are distributed, collected, and offered as an act of worship. *Fifth Sunday.* An additional opportunity to complete and offer pledge cards. On the Monday following Sunday Five, send a letter inviting those who have not yet made a pledge to do so; include a pledge card and return-addressed envelope with the letter. *Sixth Sunday.* One last opportunity to complete and offer pledge cards. One week after Sunday Six, make contacts with those who have not yet made a pledge. *Seventh Sunday.* Celebrate results and give thanks.
December	*Confirmation letters.* Mail confirmation letters to those who pledged with a note of thanks. Church leadership should write thank-you notes to all who made a pledge. Pastor writes thank-you notes to those who are providing substantial support, those who increased their giving substantially, and others who appear to be giving sacrificially.

As a part of your financial stewardship process, plan to focus on one or more of the groups as defined on the next page (and discussed in chapter four). Consider hosting "fellowship events" in homes with a message designed to meet people where they are. The most compelling stewardship witnesses will come from someone who used to be a part of the giving group they are addressing but has moved up the ladder.

Giving Profile	Description	Message
Tithers	Giving 10 percent or more to church and charity	Thank them and affirm your church's worthiness in receiving their support.
Proportional Givers	Have chosen to work toward tithing; calculate giving as a percentage of income	Use stewardship witness to encourage moving 1 or more percent closer to tithing. Consider a trial-tithe appeal.
Flat Contributors	Giving based on flat amount, usually divisible by twelve months or fifty-two weeks	Use comparison of other household expenses or purchases to motivate. Discuss the investment of resources in the church's ministry versus spending money on "wants" rather than "needs." Scripture suggestion: "For where your treasure is, there your heart will be also" (Matthew 6:21 NIV). What does the placement of their treasure say about the passions of their hearts?
Token Contributors	Usually plate-only offering, contributing whatever cash they have on hand	Refer to basic tenets of stewardship—first, that all gifts come from God. Invite them to consider their many blessings and offer gratitude to God.
Zero Contributors	Contributing no financial resources	Similar to token contributors; establish a culture of gratitude.

Make Stewardship Year Round: To-Do List

1. The stewardship committee and staff should spend one day together for the purposes of creating (and in subsequent years, evaluating) the year-round plan for stewardship. Discuss what worked and what could have worked better.
2. Do not attempt to do everything in the first year. Be strategic and get started. Incorporate additional ideas next year.
3. Just do it!

Chapter Ten

PREPARE TO SOAR

*Giving is what we do best. It is the air into which we were born. It is
the action that was designed into us before our birth.*
Eugene Peterson, *Run with the Horses*

Let's be honest. Giving makes no sense unless we somehow
come to believe what Eugene Peterson believes: we were born
to give. Unless we believe each of us is created by God to give,
everything in this book is simply manipulation, pressure, or
gimmicks designed to separate people from their most cher-
ished possession, their money. Peterson tells the story of watch-
ing a pair of swallows care for their three chicks. Eventually,
the parents took the chicks onto a branch and literally pushed
them off. The babies began to fly. One of the babies, however,
held on for dear life until finally, after being pecked at and bul-
lied, this last chick let go and began to fly:

> Birds have feet and can walk. Birds have talons and can
> grasp a branch securely. They can walk; they can cling. But
> *flying* is their characteristic action, and not until they fly are
> they living at their best, gracefully and beautifully.
> Giving is what we do best. It is the air into which we were
> born. It is the action that was designed into us before our
> birth.[1]

113

We were born to give, born to share in the nature of God, and God's most basic nature is generous giving. We believe the most powerful stewardship Scripture is the one memorized by most Christians: "For God so loved the world that he gave" (John 3:16). In an article entitled "How Much is Too Much to Give to Charity?" published in *O Magazine* in December 2009, A. J. Jacobs, a self-confessed agnostic, suggests we are born to give. In the midst of writing his book *The Year of Living Biblically*, Jacobs realized that if he was going to write a book about living one year according to the laws of the Bible, he needed to tithe. After convincing his rather reluctant spouse to give away 10 percent of their income, he began to research the charities they would support. He describes getting ready to hit the send button for giving his tithe away online: "My palms got wet, my heart rate spiked." For Jacobs and his wife, this giving would be sacrificial and require changes in their lifestyle. As the confirmation e-mails began to arrive in his inbox, he said,

> I felt good. There's a haunting line from the movie *Chariots of Fire*. It's spoken by Ian Charleson, who plays a deeply religious sprinter in the 1924 Olympics. He says: "When I run, I feel His pleasure." And as I gave away money, I think I might have felt God's pleasure. Which is odd. Because I'm agnostic. I don't know if there's a God or not, but still I felt some higher sense of purpose. It was like a cozy ember that started at the back of my neck and slowly spread its warmth through my skull. I felt like I was doing something I should have done all my life.[2]

The full quotation from *Chariots of Fire* that Jacobs refers to is this: "I believe God made me for a purpose, but He also made me fast. And when I run I feel His pleasure."[3] From Eugene Peterson, a Presbyterian pastor, to A. J. Jacobs, author and agnostic, we come together and boldly say, we are born to give.

But wait a minute. . . . If we are indeed born to give, some-body obviously didn't get the message. If one looks at the most current giving by denominations, most of us are choosing to cling to the branch and stay in the nest instead of giving and soaring as God intends.

With Methodists giving at 1.6 percent a year, Presbyterians at 1.8 percent, and Baptists at 2.6 percent, most of us are clearly not living into our birthright. Like the last baby swallow, we cling and don't want to be pushed from our comfortable nest. One preacher tells people that the big reason we don't like to give is found in a deeply theological word that begins with the letter S. Of course, everyone is ready for her to proclaim SIN as the great barrier to giving. Instead, she pauses and says . . . STUFF. Somehow, we have become convinced that the real secret to happiness, the real secret to meaning and purpose, is in stuff and more stuff. We are like children before Christmas; we plead with our parents, saying, "If I can just have _____, then I know I will be happy and I will never ask for anything else." How many of us have heard those words? How many of us as adults have uttered, or at least thought, those words? A bigger house, a new job, a raise, a new computer. Our pastor who preaches about STUFF likes to tell people about her lifelong desire to own a little red convertible BMW. She was convinced that if somehow she could just buy a red convertible BMW, she would be happy. Finally, after saving and scrimping, she got her car. Every morning, she grinned from ear to ear when she opened the garage door and saw her baby. And she was happy. She was content . . . until she got the full-colored brochure about next year's model! Like the child at Christmas, her plea-sure was fleeting. There is always something else to put into the nest, and so, like the little swallow, we want to stay in the nest with our stuff.

Stuff is indeed a crucial factor in our desire to stay on the branch and in the nest. Perhaps even more significant is the word that is often found before the word *stuff*: OUR. When we believe all of our stuff is *in fact* ours, ours to do with as we please, then giving our stuff away makes no sense. If everything we have is due to our hard work and ingenuity, then why give any more than a token, or why give at all? The very first step on the journey to bountiful giving is to understand everything we have, everything we own, is a gift, a gift from God.

Consider Jim and Ann, who had just seen their last child graduate from college and were now free. They had plans. They were going to buy a second home on the beach, and they were going to travel. They had worked hard and put their kids through school, and now they were going to enjoy life. In fact, they were often heard saying to one another, "Now, it's our time." But something strange happened as they prepared to live the high life. Somehow, they agreed to lead their church's stewardship campaign. At the time, their giving was above average but not monumental. They rarely discussed their giving and certainly never prayed about it. But during the stewardship campaign, their pastor quoted Luke 12:48: "From everyone to whom much has been given, much will be required." For the first time in their lives, Jim and Ann began to consider all they had: their house, kids, careers. All of it was given to them by God. The beach house was put off and their trips were downsized as they began tithing for the first time in their lives.

If the story ended there, it would be the kind of story we hear and celebrate in just about every church. But about this same time, Jim and Ann became familiar with a couple of teenagers who had good hearts but checkered pasts, no real parents, and struggles with alcohol and behavioral issues. One day, the pastor invited Jim and Ann to lunch. As they enjoyed their meal, the pastor asked them to prayerfully consider becoming the foster parents of these two troubled teens. After nearly choking on their food, they agreed to consider the possibility, primarily to satisfy their pastor. A commitment to tithing was one thing, but becoming the foster parents of two troubled teens was an enormous commitment, financially and emotionally. As Jim and Ann discussed the two troubled boys, they remembered their own upbringing and parents, and how blessed they had been to be raised in a supportive and loving household. Then they remembered Luke 12:48 from the stewardship campaign: "to whom much has been given, much will be required." They called their pastor and said yes. Eventually, the two teens were adopted into Jim and Ann's family. Years later, after considerable work, worry, more prayer, and tears, the two teens became responsible young men with families of their own. Now, this lovely couple laughs at the mere idea of *our time, our stuff, our life,* and will quickly tell you the best decision they ever made was to acknowledge God as the real source of all their blessings.

In 2007, Bill Gates spoke at the commencement ceremony for Harvard University. In his address, he quoted a letter from his mother:

> My mother, who was filled with pride the day I was admitted here—never stopped pressing me to do more for others. A few days before my wedding, she hosted a bridal event, at which she read aloud a letter about marriage that she had written to Melinda. My mother was very ill with cancer at the time, but she saw one more opportunity to deliver her message, and at the close of the letter she said: "From those to whom much is given, much is expected."
>
> When you consider what those of us here in this Yard have been given—in talent, privilege, and opportunity—there is almost no limit to what the world has a right to expect from us.[4]

Fascinating that a man who has accomplished so much talks about what has been given and not what has been earned. Bill Gates has already given more than $28 billion to charity and will spend the rest of his life and 95 percent of his fortune on eradicating polio and improving the lives of impoverished children around the world.[5] One of the wealthiest men in America speaks of his wealth as a gift, a gift he is determined to give away.

Let us return to the quotation from Eugene Peterson:

> Birds have feet and can walk. Birds have talons and can grasp a branch securely. They can walk; they can cling. But *flying* is their characteristic action, and not until they fly are they living at their best, gracefully and beautifully.
>
> Giving is what we do best. It is the air into which we were born. It is the action that was designed into us before our birth.

A middle-aged couple in the heartland of America, an agnostic author in New York City, and one of the wealthiest men in the world, all soaring gracefully and beautifully—doing exactly what God designed for them from the very beginning—giving.

In the end, this book is not about helping you build a magnificent new sanctuary or balance the budget. Everything you have read in this book, every item in every To-Do List, has one purpose and one purpose alone: to help you soar, to help you and your congregation become what God intended from the beginning, a people of bountiful generosity. As Eugene Peterson's swallows teach us, we were meant to soar.

APPENDIX

We believe bountiful generosity emerges from an encounter with God through gratitude, prayer, and faith. A sample of *The Journey Begins: A Devotional Guide* is included here as an example of an additional tool that can help you and your congregation experience this amazing and transformative journey. The complete devotional guide, available at horizonstewardship.com, can be effectively used during the course of any stewardship campaign or emphasis. You may choose to make it available as a booklet or electronically via email or podcast. After reading *The Journey Begins*, one young couple revealed to us, "We had never really prayed together before, or shared devotions together. This little guide changed our marriage." Let the journey begin!

Day One

They gave Moses this account: "We went into the land to which you sent us, and it does flow with milk and honey! Here is its fruit. But the people who live there are powerful, and the cities are fortified and very large.
Numbers 13:27-28 (NIV)

We're doing what? Haven't you read the headlines? Haven't you seen the news? How can we even think about having a stewardship campaign in this kind of an economy? You must be nuts. It doesn't require a great deal of imagination to think that some of the same comments were being made to Moses after the return of the spies from their visit to the Promised Land. Even without headlines screaming disaster and twenty-four-hour news trumpeting crisis after crisis, one can almost imagine the people of Israel saying some of the very same things. *You want us to do what? You expect us to go into that land with those giants and those walls and forts? You're crazy!*

Then, as well as now, the issue was the same: faith or fear. There is the voice of the Great Tempter shouting to us words of fear: *you can't, you mustn't*—and *what if?* But that is not the only voice. If we take the time to be quiet, to turn off the news, to put down the paper we will hear another voice, the voice of one who owns all of the cattle on the hillside; the voice of one who is the Great I Am, not the small and insignificant what if.

The question, of course, is which voice will we listen to? One wise pastor said that every church has two basic committees; a Back to Egypt committee ruled by fear and anxiety and an Into the Promised Land committee ruled by faith and hope. Which committee will you serve?

Remember, God isn't asking for a decision about giving today. He is asking that you to listen to His voice.

Questions to Consider

1. When have I listened to the voice of fear over faith? What were the results?
2. When have I listened to the voice of faith over fear? What were the results?

Prayer

Thank You, God, for your calming voice of faith and hope in the midst of a world filled with fear and anxiety. Help me in the days that lie ahead to take time and listen for your voice. Give me the courage to stand on the side of faith and hope versus fear and doubt, Amen.

Day Two

Then Moses said, "I must turn aside and see this great sight and see why the bush is not burned up." When the Lord saw that he had turned aside to see, God called to him out of the bush, "Moses, Moses!" And he said, "Here I am."
Exodus 3:3-4 (NRSV)

Moses was a murderer, a run away, a shepherd, yet called by God to be one of history's greatest leaders. As this stewardship adventure begins there may have been no burning bush or voice from God, unless you count the call from your pastor, one of your directors, or an invitation to a campaign event. And yet make no mistake, no matter your background: you have been called by God to be part of this exciting adventure of faith. Just as God chose Moses, you have been chosen. Can you imagine that possibility? Can you begin to even consider that your participation in this adventure is not simply random chance, not simply a last gasp attempt to raise money? Can you believe God chose you? God called you?

Her name was Brenda. She was not the first choice of any one for her particular position on the leadership team. By all accounts except God's, Brenda was a "last resort." As the campaign developed Brenda became a driving force, not due to influence or power but simply due to her quiet willingness to listen to the voice of God. As Brenda listened and opened her heart to God she became a powerful witness to God's love and mercy. And out of profound gratitude Brenda became one of the lead givers in the campaign.

Questions to Consider

1. Do I believe that God has called me to be part of this adventure?

2. Will I take the time to listen to the voice of God in the midst of this adventure?
3. Will I be willing to say yes to the call of God?

Prayer

Thank You Lord for calling me to be part of this adventure, this adventure in faith. Help me to be open to your voice, to listen to your call, and to finally discern your will for my life. "Take my life and let it be, consecrated Lord to thee." I now pray for the rest of my church family. Help us to be open to your voice, to listen to your call, to discern your will for our lives. I pray in the name of Christ, Amen.

Day Three

> *But Moses said to the Lord, "O my Lord, I have never*
> *been eloquent, neither in the past nor even now that you have*
> *spoken to your servant; but I am slow of speech and slow of tongue."*
> Exodus 4:10 (NRSV)

Even though he was called by God, even while hearing the voice of God from the midst of a burning bush, Moses was filled with doubts and questions. In chapters three and four of Exodus, Moses offers to God no fewer than four questions or doubts: Who am I to go; who shall I say has sent me; what if they don't believe me; and finally, his slowness of speech. For each case, each question, each doubt, God provided the answer. God provided the way.

This same dynamic applies to our call to give. Everyone has a multitude of reasons not to give. There is never a good time for a stewardship campaign. There is always something more pressing, a new car, a remodeled house, braces for the kids, college to save for, and retirement to worry about. And yet as God calls us to give, as God asks us to be generous, if we listen, if we are open, God also provides the way.

Terry wept at the possibility that she might not be able to give what she thought would be a generous gift. She was faced with braces, college tuition, and a cut in her husband's pay. As she poured forth her story I simply asked her to pray and be open. As she prayed she became aware of ways that she could in fact give with generosity and joy. Terry, like many, began with all the reasons she couldn't give but also like many, she came to experience the joy of sacrifice and generosity as she looked beyond the reasons to God's abundant generosity. When God calls, God also provides.

Questions to Consider

1. What are my reasons or doubts for not fully participating in this stewardship campaign?
2. How has God provided for me in the past, even when I have had doubts?
3. Can I be open to God and trust that as he calls, he also provides?

Prayer

O God, you know the many reasons I have for not wanting to serve, for not wanting to be generous. Help me to know in my heart that you have brought me to this time and this place and you will provide what I need to accomplish your task. Help me O God to have an open heart, open eyes, and open hands. We pray in Christ, Amen.

NOTES

Chapter One: Invite God into the Mix

1. "Is Gratitude the Queen of the Virtues?" Big Questions, last modified September 18, 2012, https://www.bigquestionsonline.com /content/gratitude-queen-virtues.

2. Sharyn Jackson, "One Donor Starts Chain of 5 Kidney Transplants," *USA Today*, January 11, 2013, accessed April 26, 2013, http:// www.usatoday.com/story/news/nation/2013/01/11/donor-starts-chain -of-5-transplants/1566328/.

Chapter Two: Eliminate Secrecy Surrounding Money

1. "Affluenza," PBS, accessed April 27, 2013, http://www.pbs.org /kcts/affluenza/.

Chapter Four: Tithe One On

1. Patrick Rooney, *Religious Giving*, ed. David H. Smith (Bloomington: Indiana University Press, 2010), 5.

2. "Donors Proceed with Caution, Tithing Declines," The Barna Group, May 10, 2011, accessed April 28, 2013, http://www.barna .org/donorscause-articles/486-donors-proceed-with-caution-tithing -declines.

3. Bruce Rockwell, *Spirituality and Money: 7 Questions That Saved My Spiritual Life* (Wichita, KS: The Episcopal Network for

Stewardship, 2005), 9, available from http://www.tensstore.org/p/SAM7QTSMSL.html.

Chapter Five: Stop the Insanity

1. J. Clif Christopher, *Not Your Parents' Offering Plate* (Nashville: Abingdon Press, 2008), 28.

2. Jerold Panas, *Wit, Wisdom & Moxie: A Fundraiser's Compendium of Wrinkles, Strategies, and Admonitions That Really Work* (Smashwords Edition, 2002), Kindle e-book, sec. "Big Question."

3. Panas, *Wit, Wisdom & Moxie*, sec. "Big Question."

4. Dave Ramsey, "Teaching Tithing," Ask Dave, accessed May 4, 2013, http://www.daveramsey.com/index.cfm?event=askdave/&intContentItemI=11339.

5. For some exciting and fun ideas, check out these websites:
http://christmas.organizedhome.com/celebrate/teaching-children-give
http:/casefoundation.org/spotlight/youthgiving/teaching_kids
http:www.daveramsey.com/store/kids-teens/kids-3-12/cYOUTH-cKIDS3TO13-p1.html

Chapter Six: Thank. Ask. Repeat.

1. *Giving USA 2012: The Annual Report on Philanthropy for the Year 2011,* The Center on Philanthropy at Indiana University (Indianapolis: Purdue University Indianapolis, 2012), 11, http://www.alysterling.com/documents/GUSA2012ExecutiveSummary.pdf.

2. William G. Enright, "Is It Time for Your Congregation to Rethink Its Business Model?" *Insights on Faith and Giving,* January 2013, accessed April 29, 2013, http://philanthropy.iupui.edu/files/file/january_2013_insights.pdf

Chapter Eight: Ask the Right Question

1. Ruth Moon, "Popcorn in the Pews," *Christianity Today,* January 14, 2009, accessed May 4, 2013, http://www.christianitytoday.com /ct/2009/january/18.16.html.

2. Frederick Buechner, interview by Bob Abernethy, "Frederick Buechner Extended Interview," PBS, April 5, 2006, http://www.pbs .org/wnet/religionandethics/episodes/may-5-2006/frederick-buechner -extended-interview/15358/.

Chapter Ten: Prepare to Soar

1. Eugene Peterson, *Run with the Horses* (Downers Grove, IL: InterVarsity Press, 1983), 43.

2. A. J. Jacobs, "How Much is Too Much to Give to Charity?" *O Magazine,* December 2009, accessed May 6, 2013, http://www.oprah .com/omagazine/The-Practice-of-Tithing-AJ-Jacobs.

3. Collin Welland, *Chariots of Fire* (Burbank, CA: Columbia, 1981), videocassette.

4. Bill Gates, "Remarks of Bill Gates, Harvard Commencement 2007," *Harvard Gazette,* June 7, 2007, accessed May 6, 2013, http:// news.harvard.edu/gazette/story/2007/06/remarks-of-bill-gates-harvard -commencement-2007/.

5. Neil Tweedie, "Bill Gates interview: I have no use for money. This is God's work," *The Telegraph,* January 18, 2013, accessed May 6, 2013, http://www.telegraph.co.uk/technology/bill-gates/9812672/Bill -Gates-interview-I-have-no-use-for-money.-This-is-Gods-work.html